Lectionary Tales
For The Pulpit

Series II
Cycle B

Constance Berg

CSS Publishing Company, Inc., Lima, Ohio

Copyright © 1999 by
CSS Publishing Company, Inc.
Lima, Ohio

Scripture quotations are from the *New Revised Standard Version of the Bible*, copyright 1989 by the Division of Christian Education of the National Council of the Churches of Christ in the USA. Used by permission.

Library of Congress Cataloging-in-Publication Data

Smith, Timothy J., 1957-
    Lectionary tales for the pulpit. Series II, Cycle A / Timothy J. Smith.
        p.   cm.
    ISBN 0-7880-1217-7 (alk. paper)
    1. Homiletical illustrations. 2. Storytelling—Religious aspects—Christianity. I. Title.
BV4225.2.S55   1998
251'.08—dc21   98-9783
                                                                                                               CIP

This book is available in the following formats, listed by ISBN:
    0-7880-1370-X   Book
    0-7880-1371-8   Disk
    0-7880-1372-6   Sermon Prep

PRINTED IN U.S.A.

I dedicate this book with thanksgiving to the glory of God.

I also dedicate this work to my husband, David, whose unending love gives me strength. To my children, Kjrstin and Andrew, who give me "space" when I'm on the computer. To my parents, Dick and Hetty Doesburg, who have never failed to believe in me and my worth as a person. To my in-laws, Leno and Phyllis Berg, for being the wonderful people they are. I am blessed by my whole family!

Lastly, I dedicate this book to those who are in places and times that are difficult. I learned that it is better to be true to yourself and use God's love that is in you to be a witness to others. Remember, God created you for a purpose and will never stop loving you!

Table Of Contents

Preface

Writing stories to be used by pastors in the pulpit is a big responsibility: you never know what seed will be planted! I never turned the computer on without praying first, and stories flowed from my fingers. God's hand was in each one.

Stories mirror life. These stories are from observing people, extensive reading, research, reports, the imagination, personal experience, and from the unexplainable. These stories are for storytelling and sharing as they relate to people of all walks of life.

But these are not just sermon illustrations. They can stand alone as devotions, as inspirational stories to be shared, and as motivational pieces for talks. They are stories meant to touch the heart and soul and to strengthen faith.

God has blessed me through this project. It is my prayer that the reader and the hearer of these stories will also be blessed. "The Lord is my strength and my might; he has become my salvation" (Psalm 118:14).

Solo deo gloria!!

Constance Berg
Turtle Lake and Grand Forks, North Dakota

Introduction

My prayer is that you, as church professionals, will be blessed as you use these stories. But these stories need not be limited to sermon illustrations. They can be used for Bible study, devotions, motivational talks, and prayers. These stories speak to the "people in the pew" who come to church from all walks of life, from different experiences, with varied outlooks and opinions. They will inspire, touch, motivate, challenge, educate, and provoke thought.

A careful study of the passages that accompany these stories will allow the Spirit to reveal what needs to be said. It is my prayer that these stories will get certain points across as people grow in their faith journey. May God bless you as you use these stories, as you study, and as you meditate on scriptures.

Close In Heart

"I give thanks to my God always for you because of the grace of God that has been given you in Christ Jesus."
(v. 4)

Whenever I think of Katy, I think of God's perfect timing. I met Katy when I was at a very low point, and she was at a high point in her life. We were both new "outsiders" in a tiny town.

I remember so well the day I met her. I had excused myself in the restaurant and when I came back to the booth, I saw my husband talking to a woman, laughing with her. She was sitting in the booth behind him and she was mentioning how much she loved this town she had just moved to. She was very excited!

I was anything but excited. When she said, "Isn't everyone so nice here?" I couldn't help but reply, "Yeah, to each other." My bitterness and cynicism breezed past her as she continued to spout wonders. I smiled politely.

We met all over town in the next few days. We soon became friends. We traded and shared children, feeling free when we could do errands without them. We shared our hopes and our dreams. We shared fears and struggles. And we prayed together.

Katy and I called each other at least ten times a day. One needed a recipe; the other a phone number. One needed a babysitter for Friday; one for Saturday. And so it went. We were inseparable. We were "hooked at the hip" as we said.

My depression lifted. My loneliness eased. And my self-pity vanished. I began to look beyond the tiny, rural town for other friends. These new friendships gave me renewed confidence and a sense of self-esteem. Katy had started something that only got better.

But six months after we met, Katy announced she and her husband had to leave. A better job offer had enticed her husband and they would leave in three weeks. I was unashamed to share my sense of grief at her leaving.

But I was a stronger person by then. I knew she would be better off in a bigger town with more opportunities. It made me sad, but I had rediscovered myself, my strengths, and my loves. Katy's charming effects couldn't be erased.

I cried for days when she left, but I wished her well and in a way I was happy for her. I see her every now and then and it's as if we were never apart. God sent her to me when I most needed a friend, a sister in Christ.

Katy sent me a beautiful little plaque for my last birthday. It reads: "Far in miles; close in heart." Yes, we are far in miles, but God gave a friendship that will last forever. God's timing is perfect!

Marked By The Cross Of Christ Forever

"I have baptized you with water; but he will baptize you with the Holy Spirit." (v. 8)

Blaine sat in the chair, waiting for the doctor to tell him what the problem was. He had complained about headaches for a month and the doctor assured Blaine that as soon as his sinus infection cleared, he would be fine. But a strong dose of antibiotics did not make the headaches go away. A CT scan was ordered.

On the way to the scan, time seemed to move very slowly for Blaine. His body seemed to be floating above the bed as he was wheeled through the hallways. He saw his life as a flashback as the technicians methodically did their work with the machine. It was as if he was watching them on a silent screen.

His wife, who had died several years before, smiled at him through his dream. His parents were hovering at a distance beside his grandparents. How good it was to remember them!

His dream took him to his children's baptisms. One by one, he recalled as the pastor had baptized each child, assuring them that they had entered the kingdom of God and were now a part of the family of God. Blaine remembered being embarrassed at his tears as the sign of the cross was made on each child's forehead. Blaine had been so touched.

Blaine laughed at the thought. Yes, Blaine had been touched! Touched in that same way, long ago, when he himself was baptized. His parents had carried him to the baptismal font long ago, and the pastor had made a sign of the cross on Blaine's forehead, too. Blaine had entered the kingdom of God, a part of the family of God. Blaine smiled as he was wheeled back to his room. No matter what happened, God would never leave him.

The doctor interrupted his thoughts. He looked serious. The tumor was on the pituitary gland, disrupting the sinus process. It would have to be removed and the probability of malignancy was high. Blaine's heart rate was low and medications would have to be balanced. The doctor wanted to know how Blaine was feeling. "Good and bad; sad and happy." The doctor looked confused, saying he'd leave Blaine to process the diagnosis. He'd see Blaine in the morning.

Blaine smiled. Where would he even begin explaining to the good doctor?

Joseph, Our Brother

*"Rejoice always, pray without ceasing, give thanks in
all circumstances; for this is the will of God in Christ
Jesus for you." (vv. 16-18)*

Joseph Bernardin was the Archbishop of the Roman Catholic
Church in Chicago. He became a bishop when he was only 38.
After several years, he became an archbishop, only to become a
cardinal six months later.

His father, a stonecutter, died when he was six and Joseph's
mother became a seamstress. Joseph was proud that his mother
made his first cassock.

Joseph grew to have a period of self-indulgence. One day he
realized his mistake and gave away everything that would hinder
his spiritual journey. He began early morning devotions daily at 5
a.m. and adopted new habits.

In his first address to Chicago's priests, Joseph said, "We will
work and play together, fast and pray together, mourn and rejoice
together, despair and hope together, dispute and be reconciled together. You will know me as a friend, fellow priest, and bishop.
You will also know that I love you. For I am Joseph — your
brother."

Cardinal Joseph Bernardin always addressed the people with,
"I am Joseph, your brother." It became his signature statement.
Indeed, Joseph *was* like a brother to many: to priests, parishioners,
church leaders, and the unchurched. He was not pretentious; he
was direct. He was known for his honesty, forthrightness, and
integrity.

He was also known for his faith in times of adversity. One
fateful day, adversity came in the form of a diagnosis: Joseph had
cancer. Joseph immediately sought out people: he refused to be

cut off from people and his ministry. He would continue his ministry.

When he would go to Loyola University's Cancer Center, he politely refused the private entrance. Joseph, our brother, took the main entrance. While taking treatments, Joseph shared his pain, his fears, his joy, his love for his God with others in the Center. Joseph, our brother, prayed with them. Joseph, our brother, cried with them.

Seventeen months after his diagnosis — three months since he learned it was inoperable — Joseph succumbed to cancer. He died at 68, on his mother's ninety-second birthday.

His funeral was a fitting tribute to Joseph. Flowers, cards, and tears were everywhere. And in the midst of it all stood Jewish memorial candles. A fitting tribute to a brother. A fitting tribute to one who prayed with others.

May Joseph, our brother, rest in peace.

Receiving The News

"Here am I, the servant of the Lord; let it be with me according to your word." (v. 38)

I was sitting with my husband in a doctor's sterile office when I learned I was to become a mother for the first time.

"The test is positive," the doctor told us matter-of-factly. Then he proceeded to inform us of what the due date was, what to expect in the coming months, and what role he would play during the pregnancy.

It was a scene that has played itself out countless times in doctors' offices over many, many decades.

Contrast this familiar scene with the one we might imagine surrounding the angel Gabriel's announcement to Mary that she would soon be expecting her first child.

Mary was alone, and probably in the midst of her daily routine, no thought of babies on her mind. No wonder she pondered what kind of greeting this must have been when the angel said, "Greetings, favored one. The Lord is with you," then proceeded to inform her that she would become pregnant after being "overshadowed" by the power of the Holy Spirit. Ultimately, she was told, she would give birth to a son and name him Jesus, a son who would not only "become great," but would also be called the "Son of the Most High," who would "reign over the house of Jacob forever," and whose kingdom would have no end. Her son, Jesus, would not be hers alone, but would also be the Son of God and the Son of Man.

Wow! What a difference between the news of impending birth my husband and I received and the news given to Mary, the mother of our Lord. We were certainly excited, and we had many questions. Mary had just one, a question grounded more in biology than in doubt. She simply asked, "How will this be, since I am a virgin?"

When her question was answered, she was given the additional amazing news that her relative Elizabeth — thought to be barren — was already in her sixth month. Though all this news must have been overwhelming, Mary gave an amazing response, a response which gives us some idea why this young virgin was indeed "highly favored" of God, and God's choice to become the mother to the Son of God and Son of Man, the Wonderful Counselor, Mighty God, Prince of Peace, Everlasting Father.

First, Mary responded by saying, "Here am I, the servant of the Lord; let it be with me according to your word." Then, after she visited Elizabeth, Mary responded to God's news by singing what we call "the Magnificat," a song which might be said to be the most beautiful poem of praise in the entire Bible:

> *My soul proclaims the greatness of the Lord;*
> *my spirit rejoices in God my Savior;*
> *For he has looked with favor on his lowly servant.*
> *From this day all generations will call me blessed.*
> *The Almighty has done great things for me, and holy is*
> *   his name.*
> *He has mercy on those who fear him in every generation.*
> *He has shown the strength of his arm;*
> *He has scattered the proud in their conceit.*
> *He has cast down the mighty from their thrones,*
> *and has lifted up the lowly.*
> *He has filled the hungry with good things,*
> *and the rich he has sent away empty.*
> *He has come to the help of his servant Israel,*
> *for he has remembered his promise of mercy,*
> *the promise he made to our fathers,*
> *to Abraham and his children forever.*
> *Glory to the Father, and to the Son, and to the Holy*
> *   Spirit;*
> *as it was in the beginning, is now and will be forever.*
> *   Amen.*

In response to the awesome, wonderful news that she would be responsible for bearing and giving birth to the Savior, Mary said "Yes!" to God. And how!

— Lisa Swanson Faleide
Lay Assistant, Sheyenne Rural Parish

Christmas Eve/Day
Luke 2:1-20

A Mother's Thoughts

"And she gave birth to her firstborn son and wrapped him in bands of cloth, and laid him in a manger...."
(v. 7)

She held the baby to her chest, looking into his eyes. His eyes were dark, his hair was dark, and his skin was pink. He was wrinkled. He was beautiful. She carefully unfolded a bit of the blanket and peeked inside. His fingers — they were so small! His hand seemed so small against her hand. His fingernails were tiny.

And that little neck, so wrinkled, so inviting. She kissed it softly and watched her baby squirm. She studied his face. Little lines were formed around his mouth as it made little sucking motions. He wrinkled his nose and sneezed. He opened his eyes for just an instant before closing them tightly in sleep.

Those dark eyes. She had seen a glimpse of them a moment ago. They seemed so big against his little face. She couldn't wait until he would have them open for longer periods.

He was sleeping in her arms as she thought about her baby. Her tiny little baby. What would he grow up to do? What would he be like? Would he be outgoing or quiet and reserved? Would he be full of energy or cautious? Would he play boisterously or quietly? She wondered.

The only thing she knew for sure was that he was precious. Perfect. Beautiful.

He was meant for something special, she knew. Everyone was special, although she didn't feel so special nine months ago when she found out she was pregnant. She was confused, but she knew she couldn't change what had happened. She had to live with it. She would have to be strong and carry on.

Her cousin had become pregnant recently and had given her lots of advice and support. People were talking about her and at times she just wanted to hide. But she wasn't one to seek pity. She just went on with her life.

And now she had given birth to a new life. The process was painful, but as soon as her baby was placed on her chest, it was as if the pain had been erased from her mind. He was so beautiful! So sweet, crying with all his might to announce his presence.

She didn't really know how to hold him. She was so young, barely a teenager, but as soon as she held him, kissed him, and nursed him it was as if she had always known what to do. She wasn't frightened. She just took care of her baby.

And her baby would take care of her in her old age. He could make sure her future was secure. He would see to it that her destiny was favorable.

She grew tired. She needed to sleep. But not before she gave her little son a kiss on the forehead. Such a sweet baby. She called for Joseph to take the baby. Jesus, her baby. Her sweet little boy. Her life.

A Prayer Is Answered

"At that moment she came, and began to praise God and to speak about the child to all who were looking for the redemption of Israel." (v. 38)

Virginia and Ralph wanted a child. They wanted a son, as a matter of fact. They wanted a son who would grow up to be a priest. They prayed night and day for this and before long Virginia was pregnant. She prayed she would have a son and that God would fulfill her only desire.

A son was born to them. He was a beautiful boy with lots of black hair and large, dark eyes. They named him Robert and presented him for christening.

After the christening everyone gathered around and Robert was passed around the great crowd of relatives. Amid all the oohs and aahs, Virginia went to the altar and knelt. She thanked God from the bottom of her heart for her son, her sweet little boy. She vowed she would do all she could to see that Robert would love God as much as she and Ralph loved God. She stayed for a long time at the altar before joining the party.

During the years while Robert grew up, Virginia and Ralph kept their promise to God to show Robert what a godly life meant to them. They took him to church and church school. They encouraged him to go on every youth outing. They took him on mission trips. They prayed every day for their silent wish for Robert to become a priest.

One day, when Robert was fourteen, he had a vision. He dreamed he was in a foreign country, leading worship before an enormous crowd. He was speaking with passion and the people listened. He felt very good about it.

Robert spoke to his parents about his vision and they quietly told him he had to pray about it. He would have to make the decision on his own if he felt called to fulfill that dream and become a speaker, a leader, an evangelist. Silently, they hoped.

For two years they didn't hear of Robert's dream. They didn't want to push. They didn't want to influence his decision. Just because he had experienced the church did not guarantee anything. Still, they hoped. And then one day, he came to them and announced that he felt he should be a priest. He wanted to be a pastor, a leader, a speaker. He wanted to share what he knew to be the truth of God's love.

Their joy was limitless and they thanked God without ceasing. Robert graduated from college and then went to seminary, studying, practicing, and questioning. He felt strongly about his vocation and his calling to be a pastor. While everyone else in his class seemed to have a dramatic story, Robert always said his was very cut and dried, very boring.

But Virginia didn't see it that way. She knew that Robert was an answer to prayer. Finally, on the night of his graduation, Virginia and Ralph told their son their story. They gave thanks to God together. And they watched as their son became a missionary and great evangelist. And Robert grew great in his wisdom and strong in his faith and the favor of God *was* upon him.

God's Precious Gift

"In Christ we have also obtained an inheritance, having been destined according to the purpose of him who accomplishes all things according to his counsel and will, so that we, who were the first to set our hope on Christ, might live for the praise of his glory." (vv. 11-12)

Paul and Rosa had tried and tried to have a baby. Their family knew of their frustration and tried to avoid the mention of babies. Paul and Rosa were gently urged by well-meaning friends to consult fertility doctors, but they refused. Paul didn't want Rosa to have to go through invasive testing. They felt they should trust God's will to see if a child was in their future.

Rosa went to church every Sunday with prayers in her heart for a child. Her heart ached as she watched women's abdomens swell in pregnancy. She bought baby shower gifts with tears welling in her eyes. Baptismal services were especially difficult as she and Paul watched — from a distance.

Their jobs gave them the comfort to buy much of what they desired. The law firm where Paul practiced had asked him to be a junior partner. And the gowns Rosa made had a reputation for quality craftsmanship. Business was booming at her bridal shop.

Yet every month brought the disappointing realization that there was no baby yet. They continued to pray, asking for God's guidance. Then one day, Rosa went home sick. She thought it was the flu, but it stretched over two weeks. The doctor hugged her enthusiastically when she gave Rosa the news.

Rosa called Paul, then her parents and then the church. She had to let everyone know the good news. She and Paul were on top of the world. They had waited six long years for this day!

The pregnancy went well. Near the end Rosa swore her belly would burst. But Paul and Rosa were so happy, nothing seemed to bother them. The nursery was decorated. The dresser was full of baby outfits; a bin held baby toys. The crib housed an enormous teddy bear. Things were ready.

Two weeks before the baby was due, Paul and Rosa were discussing names over dinner. Should it be Richard or Thomas, after the grandfathers? Or Mary or Christina, after the grandmothers? What about Paul Junior? Or Rachel? Or Emily or Trevor or Katherine?

They couldn't decide, yet they were sure they wanted a name with meaning. Something to let the world know their gratitude. They would have to wait and see.

The time came. After 31 hours of labor, Rosa delivered a baby boy. A healthy little boy with a pink nose and jet black hair. Paul couldn't believe how tiny his feet and hands were. He felt so light in his arms! He swore he would never let go of his sweet little baby.

They hardly let him go. They wanted to see every movement, hear every noise, and feel every wiggle themselves. A steady stream of relatives held the baby and bet on whose side of the family he resembled.

When the baby was six weeks old, Rosa and Paul went to church to have him baptized. They presented him to the church family and to God. He was God's most precious gift to them. And so they named him Jonathan: "God's precious gift."

A Different Celebration

"... and they knelt down and paid him homage. Then, opening their treasure chests, they offered him gifts...."
(v. 11)

In Mexico, it's not Santa Claus who delivers gifts. And it's not December 25 that is so important. No, it's January 6 — Epiphany — that children wait for all year.

Epiphany in Mexico is called "Dia de los Santos Reyes" or "Three Kings Day." It's the day when the three wise men bring presents to deserving children. Mexican parents warn their children to behave in order to get candy. If they don't behave, a lump of coal might be found. If the child is very mischievous he or she may even get a pile of dung from the horse, elephant, and camel upon which the kings ride.

Three Kings Day really begins the night before when children parade through the town dressed as the three wise men: Caspar, Melchior, and Balthazar. Family and friends gather to eat a sweet bread in the shape of a wreath, called "pan de rosca." In the bread is hidden a small clay doll to represent the baby Jesus. Whoever gets the doll in his or her slice has the honor of hosting next year's Candlemas party, which falls forty days after Christmas and marks the end of the Christmas season. People are usually happy to get the doll in their slice.

The next morning, the children open little gifts as a reminder of the frankincense, gold, and myrrh given to baby Jesus. Gifts can often range from candy to new shoes or clothes. This is also the day when the mother of the family lifts the baby Jesus from the creche and takes it to the church to be blessed by the priest. After the blessing, the Christ Child is put away with the other creche figures and animals until next year. Only when the Christ Child is

28

put away carefully can everyone begin feasting on tamales and atole (a milk and fruit drink).

Epiphany is the day children wait for in Mexico. It is the day when the Christ Child is blessed, the day when all children celebrate!

A Beautiful Creation

"In the beginning when God created the heavens and the earth, the earth was a formless void and darkness covered the face of the deep...." (vv. 1-2)

All he saw was a dark, formless blob. A blob that he knew would one day come alive with character. Its character he didn't know yet.

Whenever Matthew sculpted, he would consider his medium. Matthew worked this way for 43 years: making something beautiful from a shapeless blob after long consideration. He was known around the world for his sculptures, all carefully fashioned in their own time.

This time, it was clay. He didn't know what he would make of it, but he loved the warm color, the cool feeling, and the challenge. Clay dried relatively quickly, so whatever he would start would have to be finished in a timely manner. He couldn't wait to begin.

But first he looked at the mound of clay. He spent hours sitting in front of the mound, just waiting. Matthew had a theory that his mediums "talked" to him. The bronze had begged him to make it into a horse. The glass was blown into the shape of a ship. The wood had beckoned to him to become a bowl. What would the clay be? What was it telling him?

Matthew touched the clay often. It was wrapped in thick plastic, but he could feel the texture. It was pliable, yet strong. It was cool. And it could be smoothed.

The day came when Matthew felt ready. He prepared his tools and began to work. He worked non-stop, shaping, pulling, smoothing. A face emerged, upon which he added a lopsided smile. The eyes were not symmetrical: one drooped a tiny bit more than the other. The eyebrows were bushy and curly. The nose was large, but not too rounded.

The hair was a challenge. Matthew wanted a hat. He mixed more clay, shaped and pulled, and finally smoothed a hat onto the head. Some hair peeked out from under it.

Tiny instruments were used to make the final corrections and details. The eyes had a sparkle in them. The right cheek had a hint of a dimple. One ear had a tiny earring in it. A lock of hair curled into the ear.

Finally, Matthew was satisfied. He had stepped back often to consider his work, but now he stood back to observe it from every angle. He could put the finishing touches on it. It was no longer a blob. No, the woman was beautiful. She had a personality. Matthew had given her a personality, some order, and details. She was beautiful!

This I Know

"But anyone united to the Lord becomes one spirit with him ... For you were bought with a price...." (vv. 17, 20)

Some knew him as not being well versed or fluent. His grammar would have made any English teacher's hair stand on end. But he had a message to share and he was going to do it the best way he could.

He climbed the three steps as if they were twenty stories high. He made it to the top and looked around. He was nervous. So nervous we could see his hands shake. His hands clutched the sides of the pulpit so hard his knuckles were white. But he was determined. He smiled at the pastor, took another fearful look at those in the congregation, and began. He shared how he came to know Christ in a real way for the very first time one day many, many years before.

He was sitting on a park bench one day, enjoying the warmth of the sun, humming a tune from somewhere in his memory. A teenager walking by stopped and said how much she liked the tune. The teenager explained that the song had made it clear to her how much God loved her even though she was about three or four years old when she first learned it. Her mother sang it to her after her bedtime story and prayer. She said she loved to hear it in church even now.

The teenager walked on, but the man was changed forever. It was just a short, innocent conversation, but it sparked an understanding that had been buried long ago. Jesus had died. But Jesus was alive. Now he could put a name to the tune!

It gave him unlimited joy to see the church so quiet, listening intently. His voice was the only sound. He stood a little taller and shared his understanding so that all might hear! "Jesus loves me, this I know!"

He began to sing the song and as he did, he swayed. His eyes were closed and tears ran down his face. He began softly in a low, hushed whisper. Then his voice became louder, clearer, and more powerful with each note. "Jesus loves me, this I know ..." He hugged himself and then he spread out his arms.

"For the Bible tells me so. Little ones to him belong. They are weak but he is strong." He cradled his arms as he sang. He clapped his hands! He put every line into action and demonstrated the beauty of that song with his voice, his expression, and his gestures.

"Yes, Jesus loves me," he continued. "Yes! Jesus loves me ..." He wasn't quite finished with the final verse when he opened his eyes and stopped to listen. The church members were up on their feet, singing, swaying, and clapping! They were singing from their hearts.

He had spoken from his heart, from his soul, and no one had missed his message. Jesus loved him! Jesus loves all of us!

Joelito's Legacy

"Get up, go to Nineveh, that great city, and proclaim to it the message that I will tell you." (v. 2)

The prophet Jonah was commanded by God to go to Nineveh; Joel Filártiga was inspired to go to Paraguay. Jonah knew the journey and its destination would not be kind; Paraguay has not been kind to Joel Filártiga. Jonah obeyed God's call and went to Nineveh, even though he knew he it would be difficult; Joel Filártiga obeyed God's call and went to Paraguay, and his life would never be the same.

Joel Filártiga is a doctor who has dedicated his practice to healing the poorest of the poor in the remote village of Ybyqui, Paraguay. His patients come in horse-drawn carts. They walk from great distances. Dr. Filártiga spends long hours attending the needs of the people — both physically and spiritually.

Dr. Filártiga knows his patients because he and his wife, Nidia, live and work among these Guaraní-speaking people. He has committed his professional life to live among the Paraguayans in this rural setting. He has also sacrificed his personal life to the Paraguayans.

Dr. Filártiga paid a huge price for his attention to the poor and sharing his beliefs. The police kidnapped his seventeen-year-old son, Joelito, and within a few hours, tortured him to death. The police felt his father could not be stopped in his effort to bring the plight of the poor to justice. It was against his beliefs for the oppressed to continue being oppressed. It was not Christian.

Joel and Nidia's grief did not silence them. They kept their son's burned, tortured, and electroshocked body on the bloody mattress upon which it was found. Those who came to offer their condolences had to see the horrors that their son had to experience.

The doctor has found a way to try to deal with his circumstances. As Dr. Filártiga suffers in his heart with the people and heals them, he draws. And draws. Through his drawings, people have raised him up to be a true defender of the poor. Through his pencil, he has shown the outside world what the poor must endure. Through his pencil, he has shared the hope in Christ.

Dr. Filártiga's personal story is shared in the book *Compassion*, by D.P. McNeill, D.A. Morrison, and H.J.M. Nouwen (Image Books Publishing, New York, 1982). The authors tell us Dr. Filártiga is a true witness to his profession and his faith: "crying out with those in pain; tending the wounds of the poor; defending the weak and daring to accuse those who violate their humanity; joining in the struggle for justice and a willingness to lay down your life for friends." Dr. Filártiga and his wife have been called to Paraguay. They will continue to share the gospel and care for the sick as long as they are able. God's will cannot be stopped.

Dr. Filártiga is sponsored by:
Interreligious Foundation for Community Organization
402 W. 145th Street
New York, NY 10031

Knowledge vs. Love

"Knowledge puffs up, but love builds up. Anyone who claims to know something does not yet have the necessary knowledge; but anyone who loves God is known by him." (vv. 1b-3)

In the beginning they seemed normal enough. They paid rent with cash, saying their house was used as a monastery for monks. The group was very polite to guests, and they practiced meticulous housekeeping, even asking those who entered to remove their shoes before entering the mansion. Not a biased group, there were male and female, rich and poor, black, Latino, and white. It was a tight-knit group, some having friendships of over twenty years.

The group had a fascination with *Star Trek, The X-Files* and the movie *E.T.* They seemed happy and peaceful, living a simple life. They were like a close family. They had in common a desire to live a peaceable life until they would die and rise to a higher level of existence. Death was not the enemy, but life itself. Death was the reward. They denounced sex, drugs, and alcohol, declaring that Jesus was their Captain. Several times they would listen to their landlord and tell him that God would work things out. They seemed quite normal.

But the group was not what it seemed. Their leader, Marshall Herff Applewhite, was intense, charming, and charismatic. At one time he had 1,000 followers. The son of a preacher, Applewhite had given up his own plans for seminary to pursue a career in music. He was consumed with cosmology, New Age, and power.

To maintain optimum control, Applewhite and his assistant experimented on the group with sleep patterns and they all consumed huge amounts of vitamins. Members had to undergo constant mental and physical drills to prepare them for "the next life," a life that would take them from this earth to outer space.

In the beginning, they seemed so normal. So tidy. So proper. But on March 22, 1997, 39 members of the Heaven's Gate cult committed suicide together. They wanted to leave their "containers" on earth for an alien vessel that would take them to their final destination: outer space. They left identification papers, wills, and an immaculate house. They followed Isaiah's words to the letter: "Set thine house in order; for thou shalt die, and not live."

It was not until their deaths that the members of the Heaven's Gate cult were able to be scrutinized in depth. The group was androgynous, and their leader and five others were castrated long before their deaths. Members were to "overcome" their humanness, their sexuality. Applewhite, it was later learned, had a near-death experience that changed his life and in 1971 checked into a hospital to be cured of his homosexuality. He wanted sexless devotion and power. Power consumed him to commit murder — 38 times.

*　　*　　*

Also on March 22, a small cottage in the French Canadian village of St. Casimir exploded, killing all five people inside. They were members of the Order of the Solar Temple. It was all carefully planned, with three tanks of propane hooked to an electric burner and a timing device. They swallowed sedatives and waited for their final destination: the star Sirius, in the constellation Canis Major.

It was Holy Week, in the twilight of the twentieth century; Hale-Bopp lit the sky and a partial eclipse was converging. It was the perfect week for an apocalypse. They all seemed so normal.

(The information in this piece was taken from numerous *Time*, CNN, and newspaper reports from across the nation.)

Epiphany 5
Mark 1:29-39

The Church Still Lives

---

*"In the morning, while it was still very dark, he got up
and went out to a deserted place, and there he prayed."
(v. 35)*

I was the only former church leader present at the closing ceremony of the tiny country church. It was a melancholy service: serious and nostalgic. It was cold and windy outside, with the shutters banging in a rhythmic fashion. The thunder stopped long enough to give the narrator a chance for a long introduction. He asked for people to share their memories. There was a steady stream who took the microphone.

Jeff told how as a little boy he would help his mother pump the organ on the last hymn. He would "have to count to three and then step on the pedal." He said it was hard work, but he felt it was such an honor. Jeff felt it was great inspiration to become the piano player for his church choir 22 years ago.

Marta was crying when she stepped up to the microphone. She remembered her grandmother, her parents, and their siblings singing in the choir. She remembered quietly playing under the choir pews, coloring with her little sister during choir practice. When she could no longer sit comfortably under the pew, she was allowed to join in the singing of the chorus. She still loves to sing, she said.

Several others came forward to share stories. Some were antics played out as children during worship, church picnics, or funerals. Some were love stories. Some were testimonies of faith.

Finally, Bruce stood up and looked around. "I appreciate all you have said here on this sad day. But there is one thing missing. I have to say that as of today, I no longer have a church. I was baptized here. My children were baptized here and my grandchildren and two great-grandchildren were baptized here. We were all confirmed here too, even the year the church steeple burned down in the lightning storm. Several of the family were married here.

"But now I am sad," he continued. "Where am I going to go to pray? To have a quiet place to think? I don't want to go 27 miles up the road to a big, fancy church. I don't want to drive thirteen miles to the nearest church where they are all stewing in family feuds. I like it right here. For the first time in 68 years, I don't have a church."

No eye was dry when he sat down. We knew what he was saying. The bishop's representative read a proclamation, said some words, and the congregation sang "Amazing Grace." We all filed out slowly and quietly.

I sat with Bruce at the picnic afterwards. He was "feeling much better," he said, and shared several humorous stories about what had happened in the church outhouse, the parking lot, and the softball field across the driveway. He left on a light note.

Three years later, Bruce bought the church building for $500 at the auction. Most of the items inside had been sold and auctioned. He bought three pews. Bruce had the church moved a quarter of a mile down the road, to the edge of his property, where it still stands. He maintains a driveway to the church, keeping the doors unlocked so anyone can go inside.

Several people stop at the church, especially in the summer when people are heading to reunions. Bruce feels it is his obligation to provide a place of rest, a place of quiet, for anyone who cares to come inside. There is a large-print Bible at the end of one of the pews. And there is a guest book.

Bruce and his wife have moved to a larger town where they joined a church, but every Saturday he is there at the tiny country church to mow the lawn or clear the snow. As long as he can, he says he will keep the little church open.

It's a place of quiet. A place of rest. A place to pray.

Something's Missing ...

"Athletes exercise self-control in all things; they do it to receive a perishable wreath, but we an imperishable one." (v. 25)

When Todd was four years old, he loved to play T-ball. In elementary school, he looked forward to Little League games more than anything else. When Todd was in high school, all he wanted was to excel at baseball.

After school, the team would practice: stretching, running, throwing, and sprinting for hours. After practice, Todd and a few others would stay and continue throwing and hitting. Saturdays would start early in the morning with a long run and practice at 8 a.m. Even Todd's girlfriend became accustomed to being dropped off after a date long before midnight. Todd had to be well rested. Todd lived for baseball and he lived to win.

Todd played well in high school and, by his senior year, a major college welcomed him with a full scholarship. He did very well. Before his senior year in college was finished, a minor league team had signed him on. He married knowing his future was secure. When children began to come years later, he was able to provide for them well materially. Todd had everything he wanted: baseball, a contract, a beautiful family, and success.

His baseball career went well for many years, accounting for much of the success of the team. His house had a room full of awards, trophies, and ribbons. Photos of Todd and other famous players lined the walls. The one with a popular actress was signed with a kiss. Even though he was away from home more than he liked, Todd felt he had everything he ever wanted.

But Todd was restless. And he was not satisfied. He spent many hours sitting in front of the picture window outside his manager's office, looking out into space, daydreaming about nothing in particular. Todd's batting average began to drop. His throws were a bit off. And his vigor started to diminish. He was in a slump.

Todd quit the team before he was fired, stating he needed rest. Friends offered the use of a cabin and Todd and his family stayed for three months, spending long hours fishing, swimming, and hiking. He remembered how to laugh. The family remembered how to be a family again.

The vacation ended and Todd made a decision: he took a job as a manager for a small-town baseball team. He wanted peace and quiet in his life. He wanted to enjoy his children and wife. He wanted to feel that he was worth something to others.

Todd's family settled in a house in the country outside the small town. Sunsets were compared and food was grown in a garden. Todd felt as if he was regaining a sense of satisfaction but something was still missing.

One night, the local pastor came around to see Todd and remind him of the upcoming church rally. Could Todd sign photographs and be on hand to help run things? The pastor smiled as he left, holding under his arm an autographed photo of Todd in a baseball uniform.

The night of the rally came. A local band played gospel music and the crowd got situated under the huge tent. The visiting preacher was introduced and he began to speak. He spoke about Jesus, about miracles, and about parables. He spoke about an empty place that Jesus had filled in his life. And he spoke about the difference there was now that he was committed to living a Christian life.

The speaker was eloquent, funny, and serious. He didn't use theatrics, just simple, straight talk about his relationship with Jesus. He told it like it was.

Todd wasn't used to that sort of talk. He looked around, nervous. He wasn't sure he wanted to be seen there, listening to this man. But Todd sensed the honesty of the man's words and he couldn't help but listen. Todd listened intently.

Todd's life changed that night 23 years ago. He remembers the feeling he had. He recalls knowing how truthful the man's words were and how much Todd identified with them. And he remembers realizing he wanted that feeling for himself.

Todd's routine included daily prayer and study. He felt better able to make important decisions after extensive prayer. He felt better able to be the man God wanted him to be. And Todd was finally able to say he had everything he wanted: a successful career, a beautiful family, and a close relationship with Jesus.

Memories

"Do not remember the former things, or consider the things of old. I am about to do a new thing...." (vv. 18-19)

Don sat at the edge of his chair and looked right past me. "I can't hear much anymore. I can't see close up, but I can see shadows." He leaned back into his chair. I wasn't sure what to say to him.

I sat very close and asked him how he was doing on this warm winter day. Did he feed birds? Did he...? I paused as he held his hand up and pointed.

"You see right behind me? That's me and my ma and pa and my sisters. I had seven sisters. Isn't that awful?"

Through my smile, I said loudly, "Well, that's a lot of sisters to deal with. I..." But he leaned forward again and interrupted me.

"I lost four of them in two winters. Hardest thing my momma had to go through. Molly fell in the molasses pit. And Virginia and Hilda fell while racing our new horses. The horses weren't broken yet and Pa had warned them not to ride them. Pa was furious and he was very sad. And then Sarah had to go and try to walk home from school during a blizzard. She told the teacher it didn't look that bad and that she'd rather ride out the storm at home in front of the fire with Mama. She only made it halfway through the field."

Don closed his eyes and leaned back. I touched his arm, not knowing what to say. Tears welled up in my eyes. I saw him dab his eyes hastily.

"I'm over it now. That's been 62 years ago. But my mother never recovered. At first people were very helpful and came by, bringing food. They helped Pa at the mill, helping him finish his work. But then Ma began to hear gossip. The townsfolk said she had done something very, very wrong for four daughters to have died so suddenly and so young.

"Some said she had an evil eye. Some said she must have done something so secret and so bad that only God could know what she had done. They said God was surely punishing her. The sheriff even asked her about her courting behavior before she married Pa. He was interested in every little thing. It really hurt Ma when he would come around asking questions like that.

"Ma never got over it. She stopped washing the clothes, then she stopped cooking, saying my other sisters had to learn anyway. After a while, she would come downstairs in her robe and sometimes she would take long naps on the davenport. It wasn't like her at all. Before my sisters died, my ma had always been so prim and proper, doting on any visitor. And the house had always been immaculate. Then it was never cleaned as well again. It was like she was believing what the people were saying.

"Then one day she started crying and then screaming. She screamed so loudly the neighbors came running, but she wouldn't let them in the house. They said she was breaking things and carrying on.

"The sheriff knocked down the door and tied her hands behind her back. I was just coming home from school when they took her away. The neighbors said they had been right all along. She had done something and now it was coming out. They said she couldn't hide anything from them.

"I never saw my mother again. We got a letter two weeks later saying she had been taken to a sanitarium 200 miles away. Then four months later, they sent us a death notice, but there was no reason given. I think she died of a broken heart."

Don closed his eyes and began to snore softly. The sound of my sobbing was the only sound in the room. I stayed a minute. I needed to compose myself.

Forgiven And Encouraged

"Jesus said to them: 'Those who are well have no need of a physician, but those who are sick; I have come to call not the righteous, but sinners.' " (v. 17)

Lee and JoAnn had foster children in their homes for years. Fifteen children came and went through their twenty years of marriage — along with three sons of their own. Then they heard about Jon.

To be more exact, they heard about Julie, a ten-year-old who had been beaten and molested as she walked home from school. Jon had been with the two older boys who initiated the crime. Jon had been taken along to "watch and learn."

But Jon was only thirteen years old. And twelve and a half of those thirteen years had been spent in foster homes. Because he was so young, Jon was sentenced to home confinement until he was eighteen. JoAnn and Lee asked the court to have Jon in their home.

Jon came immediately; the judge was very relieved to have a home for him. And JoAnn and Lee began a new chapter in their life. They still had three foster children in their home: twin boys of ten and another boy of seventeen.

The family sat down and explained the daily routine, including the chores and responsibilities expected of each child. They explained to Jon that every act would have a consequence. Jon would be in charge of his destiny — either by reward or punishment.

It took the first hour for Jon to understand the seriousness of each family member's role. He didn't feel like washing the dishes, so the younger children couldn't dry and clean up and play outside. Jon felt like watching television. His television privilege was taken away for a week.

45

After washing the dishes, Jon got into an argument with the seventeen-year-old and punched him. Jon's bike would be locked up for two days. He would have to walk the mile and a half to school.

The family had another meeting before bedtime that first night and Jon was asked if he understood the family structure. He understood the system and his part in it. He would have to learn to cooperate to keep the family going. Everyone would be allowed to try again the next day.

The first week was very difficult as each son sized up Jon. They tested each other to the limit and each time they understood the consequence they faced. They also understood that they were forgiven and encouraged to try yet again.

The first year went by with many trials, but JoAnn, Lee, and the boys came to an understanding: they would have to get along because they had to live together for a long time. The seventeen-year-old turned eighteen and was taken to college amid cries and hugs. Jon was now the oldest and in charge. He had to learn to delegate, supervise, and help. He learned to rely on his younger brothers and also to take care of them. He learned many things in the next years.

Jon stayed with JoAnn and Lee many years. During those years, he came to understand that he was a valued member of the family. He learned to be responsible for his actions. And he learned that when he made a mistake, he had to be accountable and would be allowed to try again. He knew the definition of forgiveness.

Saint Thomas Aquinas

"For it is the God who said, 'Let the light shine out of darkness,' who has shone in our hearts to give the light of the knowledge of the glory of God in the face of Jesus Christ." (v. 6)

Thomas Aquinas, the great philosopher, theologian, and teacher, is the patron saint of Roman Catholic universities, colleges, and schools.

Thomas Aquinas, born in the mid-1220s, was the son of Count Landulph of Aquino and Countess Theodora of Teano. He was related to the Emperors Henry VI and Frederick. Thomas could have been destined for fame through the military or royalty. But a "holy hermit" had predicted that this young boy was going to be a preacher and have learning and teaching so great that no one could even come close to his scholarly excellence. And his personal devotion and lifestyle would be above reproach by anyone.

The hermit's words came true. At an early age Thomas was sent to learn from the Benedictine monks. This was customary in those days. It is said he was witty, precocious, and had thoughtfulness above his years. Many writings attest that he learned with ease because he had perfect recall. He also never began his studies until he prayed in earnest. He surpassed his teachers with his knowledge and insight into the lessons.

The religious life was what Thomas wanted more than anything. The city fathers could not understand that a nobleman should become a priest. His mother was also confused, sending Thomas' brothers to kidnap him. He was imprisoned for two years while his family tried to change his mind. They even tried to tempt him with a woman. But Thomas evicted her from his chambers and asked God to grant him integrity of body and of mind. When he was asleep he had a vision that angels gave him a girdle of virginity.

His mother seemed to understand Thomas' seriousness about his vocation. As soon as he was freed, he was sent to Rome by the Dominican brothers. They were thrilled that during his imprisonment Thomas had memorized scriptures and had solidified his vocational desire. He was sent to learn and teach in various places, amazing the teachers and students with his humility and knowledge.

Thomas gave up the chance for nobility for the life of a monk, dedicating his learning to teaching, writing, and defending the Christian truth. He tearfully turned down the offer to become archbishop of Naples, his birthplace. He felt he wasn't good enough and he wanted to remain a monk. His greatest writing, *Summa Theologica*, instructed theology students with a summary of Christian philosophy.

Thomas Aquinas died in 1274 after being convinced that he would receive no more holy visions. He was canonized in 1323 and in 1880 was named the patron saint of Roman Catholic institutions of learning.

May God bless us as we consider emulating the dedication of Saint Thomas Aquinas.

Ash Wednesday
Matthew 6:1-6, 16-21

Treasures

"For where your treasure is, there your heart will be also." (v. 21)

A man bought a house. It was a three-bedroom house with a nice, large kitchen, a den, and a living room. The backyard was tiny, but it was filled with flowers neatly placed around the perimeter. The couple had no children and spent their weekends boating at the lake or going to the desert or mountains.

They had a peaceful life.

The man's wife liked jewelry and whenever she saved up a hundred dollars or so from her grocery coupons, she would buy herself a trinket — a gold necklace, a sapphire ring, a ruby bracelet. She loved her jewelry; they were her little treasures on earth. She spent lots of hours cleaning and polishing and storing her treasures.

The husband bought her a fancy jewelry box. This way his wife could have all her prized possessions in one place. More rings, bracelets, and necklaces filled the box to capacity. Soon, he bought her a jewelry armoire.

Then there were a few robberies in the neighborhood. The couple decided they had too many cherished items to have their house vulnerable in their absence. The man bought a home alarm system.

Now when they go out, they have to put in several numbers to activate security cameras. When they come home, they have 45 seconds to walk through the door and punch in a complex code so the alarm won't go off. Their life is not so peaceful anymore.

"For where your treasure is, there your heart will be also."

Baptism

---

*"And baptism ... now saves you — not as a removal of
dirt from the body, but as an appeal to God for a good
conscience...." (v. 21)*

"Oh, Mom, don't be silly. I don't need Erin baptized. I don't
go to church and I would be two-faced if I only came to have her
baptized."

Judy's eyes welled up with tears. Caroline's words stung. She
may as well have been slapped. She couldn't force her daughter to
bring her baby to church to be baptized; it was Caroline's decision
to make. She never brought up the issue again.

Erin grew up to be a beautiful girl: gentle, smart, and caring.
She was strong-willed and beyond her years in maturity. At twenty,
she spent more hours at the mission feeding the homeless than
studying. But her top grades seemed to come to her without much
effort. She was compassionate. And unbaptized. It broke Judy's
heart that her only grandchild was not baptized, but it was not her
place to bring it up again.

The day came when Erin married a charismatic professor who
loved nature and the outdoors more than anything else. And he
was a Christian. Erin and Tom had many discussions about children, wanting to start their family as soon as they were able. Erin
and Tom had three children in five years. And none was baptized.

They had many arguments over baptism. Erin didn't subscribe
to putting on appearances; Tom didn't want to force his convic-
tions on Erin. They agreed to disagree. They dropped the subject
of baptism.

Then Judy became terminally ill. She gathered her daughter
and granddaughter around her and explained her illness to them.

They cried together as they considered the injustice of it: they were the only family they had. But Judy made them laugh, recalling how Caroline would steal her mother's broom so she could play horsy. How Erin would toddle up to her gramma and ask her for just one more bedtime story long after she should have been asleep.

The three of them spent many long hours together until Judy's death. Caroline found a set of Judy's journals. Eighteen books told of Judy's heartaches, joys, triumphs, and trials. The last held letters telling Caroline about Judy's belief in God, Judy's absolute assurance of being a child of God.

Caroline read of her own baptism, the day Judy had brought her to the church in front of family and friends. That day Caroline was assured that she was a child of God too.

"God came to you that day, Caroline. No matter what you have done, no matter what you have thought, no matter what you have not done, God has been with you. That day of your baptism opened the door to heaven for you. It was the day the Holy Spirit entered your life, never to leave. It was the first day you took a step toward heaven in your journey in life. It was the happiest day of my life."

It took several weeks for Caroline to gather the courage to share the diaries with Erin. She felt she had a reawakening, another beginning, a baptism of sorts. And suddenly it was too important to ignore. Too important not to share it with her daughter and grandchildren. Caroline and Erin and Tom spent days talking about life, about God, and about faith.

Life was too precious not to include God. Erin and her children were baptized five months later.

Every Child Has A Purpose

―――――――――

*"No distrust made him waver concerning the promise
of God, but he grew strong in his faith as he gave glory
to God." (v. 20)*

It was Alpha's eightieth birthday and the party was grand.
Relatives, friends, and neighbors came to celebrate the day with
her. The porch, sunroom, and backyard were full of well-wishers.
The tables along the back of the house were heavy with meats,
sandwiches, salads, and desserts. Alpha thought it was an elabo-
rate affair. She was having fun.

Evening came and a few of Alpha's children stayed around.
They had had so much fun planning the surprise and their efforts
had been well rewarded. All the children and their families had
come.

All except one. Kimmie's absence wasn't mentioned, but Alpha always missed her when the family got together. Kimmie had
been gone ten years now. Alpha knew in her heart that when her
husband died soon after, it was of a broken heart. They had been
through so much with Kimmie. Her drowning was the last straw
for him.

Alpha remembered the day of Kimmie's birth 33 years ago
like it was yesterday. Alpha and Dick thought their family was
complete, but at the age of 47, Alpha gave birth to Kimberly Marie.
She was a sweet little girl with almond-shaped eyes. She had short,
stubby little fingers and toes. They called her Kimmie.

Alpha and Dick took her home. Her brothers and sisters were
so excited with Kimmie. They were much older than Kimmie and
were very protective of her. When Kimmie was five, Alpha noticed that Kimmie didn't seem to advance like the others. Maybe

Kimmie's just a little slower, she thought. But when they took her in for the kindergarten evaluation, Alpha and Dick got the news: Kimmie had Down Syndrome and very mild mental retardation.

Alpha didn't really know what that meant at the time, other than that Kimmie would always be slower. As the years progressed, however, she and Dick came to realize that Kimmie required special teachers, more patience, and closer supervision.

Alpha spent the next twelve years fighting for special education and then mainstream programs. She spoke to the schools, local leaders, and finally to Congress until programs were started, funding was put into place, and changes were made. Alpha realized if it hadn't been for Kimmie's birth, she would never have been aware of the needs of children with special needs. She and Dick had the chance to see many, many advances in the area.

At a graduation, Alpha had spoken to the students about Kimmie's first days of kindergarten, the special education classes, and finally the mainstreamed high school classes. She spoke to the parents of the many highs and lows of her life. And she repeated the words of her doctor so long ago: "Every child is precious, every child has a purpose, but Kimmie's life is destined to change other's lives." Indeed, Kimmie's existence had turned out to benefit all.

The Portrait

———

> *"For the message about the cross is foolishness to those who are perishing, but to us who are being saved it is the power of God." (v. 18)*

Paul couldn't stand it anymore. The constant ringing in his ears was deafening. It was as if he were standing in the ocean, the waves pounding unceasingly in his ears. He knew he was going deaf quickly.

Paul's hearing loss came rapidly. The doctors tried hearing aids. But nothing made the ringing stop. And nothing made the noise of normalcy return.

Paul became depressed and withdrawn. He couldn't understand what people were saying. Normal activities like grocery shopping and driving became a terrifying ordeal. It was easier to stay home and retreat into his world of silence.

People didn't know what to do with Paul. Some came to visit, but writing compassionate little comments got tiring for them. It was too frustrating. Others would send inspiring cards, but the words seemed empty. They couldn't touch his cold heart.

Paul turned to his art for solace. He would sketch on his sunny porch. He would draw in the living room by the picture window, watching the children play in the park across the street. He would sit in the park and think of new ideas.

In time, Paul began to feel more alive. He began to paint faces, and soon he would sit and sketch portraits for free. As soon as he would come to the park, he would have a gathering. It was his pleasure to see the surprised, happy faces of his "models." He was coming out of his shell. The people understood he was deaf. The people understood he had talent.

Paul was asked to sketch a portrait of Jesus for the church across town. The pastor had come to watch Paul. Paul had sketched the pastor's daughter in an amazing likeness the week before. Pastor Tim sat with Paul and wrote his request.

Paul was quick to shake his head no. He was adamant. But Pastor Tim was adamant too, and asked if Paul would "just come and take a look at our church." It was a new sanctuary built behind the original, ancient church and Pastor Tim wanted a fresh, modern look. He wanted a portrait of Jesus in the narthex.

Pastor Tim left Paul with the address, which Paul ignored for three weeks. But curiosity got the best of him. Paul headed across town.

Paul's world was one of silence; it helped him concentrate. Paul's world was one of a loner; it helped him notice details. Paul's world was one of introspection; his intuition was keen.

Paul sat in the church for hours on end, days at a time. He wanted to get a feeling of this Jesus. He wanted an idea for a sketch to come to him. He wanted an image to form in his mind so he could begin to sketch. He wanted something concrete.

But nothing came to him and just as he was about to give up, he heard a voice in the silence. It wasn't an audible voice. It was a quiet voice only for Paul to hear. It was the voice of one who had suffered. It was the voice of one who understood. It was the voice of one who wanted to love.

Paul practically sprinted home. He got out a huge canvas, clean and bright. And on it he painted a face. A face that was neither male nor female. A face that was neither black nor white. A face that was neither happy nor sad.

It was a lonely face. A caring face. An authoritative face. It looked pensive. It looked knowledgeable. It looked curious.

After a month of daily work, Paul was finally satisfied with it. But as he stood back, he realized he had forgotten the most important detail. Jesus' reason for coming to earth was missing. On the side of his face, on the curve of his cheekbone, Paul painted a tiny tear. A tear of happiness. A tear of sadness. A tear of understanding.

Paul was finished. He had heard the voice. Paul understood.

Life's Purpose

*"For we are what he has made us, created in Christ
Jesus for good works, which God prepared beforehand
to be our way of life." (v. 10)*

Holly was washing the dishes, listening to her favorite gospel quartet on tape, when two men pulled up the driveway and came up the walk. They identified themselves as Federal Bureau of Investigation officers and asked Holly for her identification. They asked to come inside.

They were very polite when they asked about her husband's assets. Holly shared with them that she had questioned Jeff in the beginning about the steady stream of "toys" he brought home. But Jeff was so charming and he had convinced her that he was rewarded with perks for being such a great salesman. Holly showed them little notes that had come with the "perks" — each one professing Jeff's talent at sales.

At first the "bonuses" were T-shirts — then silk neckties. Then they turned into fine grain leather boots and an onyx ring. A full-length leather coat was followed by leather suitcases. Soon the "perks" turned into trips, a fishing boat, and a new sports car. Jeff brought home a reasonable paycheck but bragged how these "benefits" made his dull job exciting. Holly always felt God had taken such good care of them through the years.

The officers were very kind to Holly as they questioned her. They asked to see the garage, the three sports cars, Jeff's jewelry, and the mink coat. They made lengthy notations in a notebook.

The men spoke slowly and looked Holly straight in the eye. They asked her point-blank how Jeff had accumulated such extravagant items on a mid-range salary. Then they told her: they had proof that Jeff had embezzled at least $800,000 from the company. Holly felt faint and nauseous. She was in shock.

Jeff didn't come home that night. Instead, he called her three days later, saying he had gone to another country and "she should go on without him." He told her he had made a very big mistake, that he was about to be caught and needed to leave. Jeff told Holly he loved her.

It took Holly three months to realize Jeff was gone forever. And it took as long to convince the banks to change papers and possessions into her name. Holly was dulled and moved as if by remote control. She lacked energy, but she found inner strength: she was five months pregnant.

Holly moved into an apartment, then three years later moved into a small house. She made a comfortable life for her little son. When her son was seven, she married a man who adored her, a man who loved her son.

Her new husband, Bill, wanted children desperately and by their third anniversary they had two girls. They were ecstatic, yet their joy was short-lived. Their youngest got leukemia and died on her second birthday.

But Holly and Bill continued to live life and trust in God. The years after their daughter's death were painful and difficult, but they concentrated on their two other children and made a good life for them. Holly's happiest days were watching her children graduate from graduate school and high school in the same week.

She loves Bill and feels God truly comforted her during her difficult periods in life. They feel they can survive if they hold close to their faith and each other. They know God has a purpose for their life.

A Blessed Harvest

*"Unless a grain of wheat falls into the earth and dies,
it remains just a single grain; but if it dies, it bears
much fruit ... Whoever serves me must follow me, and
where I am, there will my servant be also. Whoever
serves me, the Father will honor." (vv. 24, 26)*

It sounded like thunder. There wasn't a cloud in the sky that morning. The noise grew louder. The earth seemed to vibrate.

Nine long grain trucks, several farm trucks, a fuel truck, seven enormous combines, and numerous cars rumbled down the highway. This was obviously a procession. A procession with a mission.

This was the day of the harvest bee at the Swensen farm. Thelma had had a stroke again and wasn't showing much progress. Harry wasn't very steady on his feet anymore since his hip surgery last month. A few friends had called each other and decided to help Thelma and Harry out. They called some others.

The group had gotten an early start. The weather was being cooperative and the wheat was ready. Thermoses and water jugs were filled. Everyone had a job to do.

They worked through the morning. At noon, it took the women an hour to set up tables with food; it took thirty minutes for it all to be eaten. Hot dishes, salads, breads, and cookies were devoured without ceremony.

This group lived in the same area. They were all neighbors and most were farmers. The weather couldn't have been more perfect: not too wet, not too dry. It would be a bumper crop for most. It was certainly a bumper crop for Harry.

This had all come about because last Sunday the pastor announced in church that Thelma had suffered another stroke. The men had gathered outside after church to share harvesting stories when one of them mentioned he would swing by to see if Harry needed help. Another said he'd join him and then there was a chorus of volunteers. Soon there was a small army formed to take on Harry's crop. It had been planned in a matter of minutes. It didn't take long for the news of the plans to spread.

At the end of a long day the engines finally stopped. Sandwiches, salads, and cookies were served again. A hush came over the group. There was nothing much to say. The harvest had gone smoothly. Everyone had known what to do.

It seemed like a small effort for each one. Only one day out of their lives. Just one day to help Harry. One day to be a helpful neighbor. One day to be a witness.

The fieldwork was finished; their relationships weren't. God had blessed their community. God had blessed their harvest.

Julia

"... but emptied himself, taking the form of a slave, being born in human likeness. And being found in human form, he humbled himself and became obedient to the point of death — even death on a cross." (vv. 7-8)

Julia is the first of seven children and the only girl. She rises early in the morning to pick vegetables, grind corn, and begin the process of preparing breakfast. She does not go to school; she tends to the home so her brothers can go. Her mother has aged beyond her 28 years, moving slowly, waiting for her eighth child to be born.

Julia lives in the highlands of central South America. She is ten years old, loves to draw, and loves to listen to her transistor radio. She fantasizes often about the songs she hears, wondering what it would be like to live in a city, to have running water, and to have lots of friends. Her mountain village is only accessible by foot or cart and donkey.

She traveled once to the city three hours away when she was sick. She was too ill to remember the journey. Julia had a dark spot on her leg, just above her knee. Then she got a boil. The local midwife lanced it, but it became infected. The wound festered and soon encompassed her entire thigh. She was taken to the city. The doctors took one look at her, told her she had a tick inside her leg and took her to surgery. Eight hours later, she woke up in excruciating pain with her leg amputated just below the hip. That was two years ago.

When Julia was in the hospital, the nurses befriended her. They introduced her to a Christian woman, Becky, who had three daughters. The girls visited Julia often and helped distract her when the pain was unbearable. Julia had to remain in the city for three months, living with her new friends.

Becky made no apology in telling Julia about Jesus — about a cross, about sacrifice, and about hope. It fascinated Julia. Why would anyone want to have a son and choose to see him die? There were days when Julia wanted to die, but her mother wouldn't have felt the same. Julia asked Becky many questions.

When the rehabilitation time was finished, Julia made plans to return to her village. But she knew things would never be the same. She was riding out her time until the day she could return to the big city. Julia was going to work for the church, teaching children. She knew in her heart that was what she was going to do.

It's very difficult to walk on the mountainous terrain with only one leg, but Julia doesn't complain too much. She knows she'll never marry because in her village a woman's worth is equal to the work she can accomplish. And Julia can hardly carry anything.

Even though she is only ten, Julia is much older than her age. She cares for her younger brothers and helps her mother as best she can. Julia hopes she will have a baby sister who will one day grow up to help her around the house.

Every day she wakes up early in her village to pick vegetables, grind corn, and begin preparing breakfast. She will do what is expected of her. She will help out until she is old enough to leave. It's worth it. She has a future to wait for.

Madame And Maid

---

*"So if I, your Lord and Teacher, have washed your feet,
you also ought to wash one another's feet. For I have
set you an example...." (vv. 14-15)*

Isabel put on a white glove. Today was Thursday. Cleaning day in the house. She always checked behind Keera to see if any dust was left behind.

She led her gloved finger over the mantel, onto the picture frames, behind the bust of Beethoven, between the piano keys. No dust. She ringed the lamp shade, poked under the bed frame, around the kitchen lights. Still no dust. She was satisfied.

Isabel asked when supper would be served. She got situated on the couch and put her feet on the ottoman. She reached for the remote and turned on the evening news. It felt good to sit down after a long day at the firm. This was her favorite time of day. She closed her eyes.

Keera brought in a small tray of hors d'oeuvres. Keera had been with Madame for seven years now, as soon as Keera was old enough to work alone. Keera's mother had trained her well; when Keera turned ten, her cousin took her along on cleaning jobs whenever she could.

Many maids came and went in Madame's mansion. It was enormous, but the staff was well-trained and meticulous. Keera began as a maid's assistant in the kitchen and quickly worked up to first maid. She loved it, even though it was very difficult work. But "Madame," as she was called by the staff, had been very patient with Keera.

Keera was very intelligent. Keera loved watching panel discussions, debates, and interviews. She had a passion for news. When she first came to Madame's house, she asked for permission to wear a personal radio during her cleaning chores. Madame agreed on the condition that Keera's work be without fault.

Then a ritual started. Keera would help Madame lay out the next day's clothes and prepare her bath and Keera and Madame would "discuss." At first it was polite talk, with Keera doing the listening. But soon it turned to debate, discussion, arguing, and questioning. Keera listened carefully to the news and asked Madame about details which were not reported. She had a very keen mind.

Theirs was a strange friendship. To the public, they were Madame and Maid. But they looked forward to the nightly debates, sometimes heated. Madame tested many of her cases on Keera, asking Keera how she would interpret certain testimonies.

There were times when Keera would wonder why she had to work so hard but Keera knew the more regular Madame's life was, the better it was for everyone. Keera's life wasn't made of titles or wealth, but it was a good life.

An Hour To Think

"But he was wounded for our transgressions, crushed for our iniquities; upon him was the punishment that made us whole, and by his bruises we are healed." (v. 5)

Tim wanted to get home. It would be so good to see Meg and the children again. It had been five days since his business trip began. He was so eager to get home.

Tim left the office early today. After the short plane ride earlier that morning, he would have loved to skip the office, but he needed to update the boss.

He wanted to get home so they could all go to the Good Friday service. He liked that service. Meg thought it was depressing and went to please Tim. But Tim liked it. It was calming for him. Easter services were always so chaotic and he didn't like all that commotion. He liked low-key things.

Tim was daydreaming as he rode home the last half hour of the drive. He wasn't really paying attention when suddenly his car swerved, nearly skidding off the road. He pulled over and got out. What was that noise? It sounded like a shot. He circled the car and kicked it when he saw the right front tire, flat as a dime. He instantly regretted his action. He was so grateful he didn't hit anyone. He was so glad he was in the outside lane. He thanked God under his breath for safety as he took off his suit jacket and opened his trunk. It took him an hour to get everything out of the trunk, change the tire, and put the stuff back in. Next week he'd have to clean out that trunk.

He looked at his watch. Too late to catch church with his family. He didn't feel like walking in in the middle of the service. Then he had an idea. He would go to the church across the way.

Tim slipped in quietly. Silence greeted him like a warm blanket. It was just the thing he needed. He sat in the fourth pew toward the center. He looked around, awestruck once again by his surroundings.

He knew this cathedral quite well; he had designed its new narthex. It was a magnificent structure with wings everywhere. The original church had been built over a hundred years ago. It had high ceilings, painted in the center dome. The stations of the cross were carved from wood. The statues gleamed in the low light. It was such a peaceful place.

The altar had been stripped. The fire had been extinguished. The paschal candle stood ready at the side of the altar.

Tim closed his eyes. He welcomed the silence that surrounded him. It was so good to sit in a hushed place. The quiet overtook him.

He opened his eyes and looked at the cross. It was a new one. He had heard about it. It had been carved in Montana and it looked rustic yet elegant. It was simple at a glance, but intricate carvings inside the arms defied description. They were very detailed. It was a beautiful cross.

Across the crosspiece were curves. Were they arms? A curve dipped at the center. Was it a place for a head? Tim knew that wasn't an accident. The carver was a master of the craft.

What was it like to die on a cross? It had to be horribly painful. It had to be terribly excruciating. But it had to be.

Tim thought about that for a while. What was it like for Jesus to walk up toward the cross, knowing he would have to be beaten, hanged, and killed? Yet knowing he would rise again. Wasn't that scary? Wasn't it wonderful? It had to be the worst and best of anything anyone could imagine. Tim certainly couldn't imagine what it would be like.

Tim heard a stirring behind him as a woman sat down at the back of the church. He looked at his watch. An hour had gone by. An hour. An hour of quiet. An hour of tranquility. An hour of undeniable peace.

Easter
Acts 10:34-43

"Christ Jesus Lay In Death's Strong Bands"

"They put him to death by hanging him on a tree; but God raised him on the third day and allowed him to appear ... after he rose from the dead." (v. 39-41)

Christ Jesus lay in death's strong bands
For our offenses given;
But now at God's right hand he stands
And brings us life from heaven.
Therefore let us joyful be
And sing to God right thankfully
Loud songs of hallelujah!
Hallelujah!
It was a strange and dreadful strife
When life and death contended;
The victory remained with life,
The reign of death was ended.
Holy Scripture plainly says
That death is swallowed up by death,
Its sting is lost forever.
Hallelujah!
Here the true Paschal Lamb we see,
Whom God so freely gave us;
He died on the accursed tree —
So strong his love — to save us.
See, his blood now marks our door;
Faith points to it; death passes o'er,
And Satan cannot harm us.
Hallelujah!
So let us keep the festival
To which the Lord invites us;

Christ is himself the joy of all,
The sun that warms and lights us.
Now his grace to us imparts
Eternal sunshine to our hearts;
The night of sin is ended.
Hallelujah!
Then let us feast this Easter Day
On Christ, the bread of heaven;
The Word of grace has purged away
The old and evil leaven.
Christ alone our souls will feed;
He is our meat and drink indeed;
Faith lives upon no other!
Hallelujah!

> — Martin Luther (1483-1546)
> *Lutheran Book of Worship* #134

Peace Be With You

"Jesus came and stood among them and said, 'Peace be with you.' " (v. 19)

"Peace be with you. Peace be with you."

Handshakes were shared around the sanctuary. Many people hugged. Some slapped a "high-five" while others started chitchatting. "Peace be with you" echoed throughout the church.

But just outside the church was another world. A world where gangs hung out. More accurately, one gang hung out in the church alley. Other gangs were chased away. It was not strange to hear gunshots in the night. It was not uncommon to hear of drive-by shootings. It was all too often that funerals included innocent victims of gang rivalry.

This was life outside the walls of St. Mark's. It was punctuated by violence, oppression, and poverty. Most of the parishioners were former gang members. Many were single parents. Most children belonged to the neighborhood gang. And everyone respected the power of the gang's potential.

The potential for violence was everywhere in this area. What was once a middle-class neighborhood of immigrants working at the shipyards was now a run-down area where drug dealers worked. Teen pregnancy was accepted as the norm. Welfare was a fact of life.

People who weren't from this area avoided it like the plague. They didn't know the inner workings. They didn't know who did what. They just stayed away.

But not Pastor Jerry. He had come twelve years ago and was still there. He didn't like the violence and spoke out against it as often as he could. But he also understood economics, pride, and loyalty. He understood the language of the inner city.

It was not a peaceful area, but the inside of the church was sacred. He did not tolerate hats, bandanas, offensive clothing, weapons, or disrespect inside his church. The first year was difficult as he gently told children that they were welcome but they would have to return home to change clothes if they wanted to attend worship service. His windows were broken out many times. His tires were slashed routinely. But he wouldn't budge. The church would not be a place of this kind of behavior.

And it worked. Word got out that Pastor Jerry didn't put up with certain things. When people entered this church, there was quiet. There was respect. It was sacred ground.

Blooming

"Beloved, we are God's children now; what we will be has not yet been revealed." (v. 2)

"You know how three weeks ago I asked you to speak about your trip to Mexico? Well, could you talk about flowers instead?"

It was only 24 hours before I was to speak at a Mother-Daughter banquet. I cringed. I knew nothing about flowers. My meditation time tripled the next morning.

I cried out to God. What could I say about flowers, for heaven's sake? And how could the topic be changed at the last minute? I had wanted to be inspirational and knowledgeable when I spoke and I was looking forward to speaking about my favorite subject — Mexico — my favorite place on the planet. And now I had to speak about *flowers*! There had to be a reason.

God was more than gracious. During my quiet time that morning I remembered the beautiful orchids growing wild in the jungles. I recalled walking to my preaching assignments in the Guatemalan jungle and seeing breathtaking visions of the most exquisite flowers one could imagine. I'd have to sneak that into my talk.

Then I recalled words that my mother had told me umpteen times when I was young — blossom into a beautiful flower no matter where you are, no matter who you are with, and no matter what the situation — an extended version of Dr. Norman Vincent Peale's famous "Bloom Where You Are Planted" sentiment. I would make my speech around this point.

My Bible reading was about trusting God and being a child of God. A topic of flowers had reduced me to a fearful child and now the answer lay in scripture. God must be wanting to talk through me, I decided.

I ventured out with my six-year-old daughter and found the church in the small town about fifty miles away. We walked in and people welcomed us warmly.

The hall was decorated, the tables set beautifully, and several ladies had poems and readings about flowers. The meal was delicious and served by several men who were ready to give us anything we needed. Dessert came and suddenly my stomach was in my knees as I quivered and wondered if I was prepared. Would I stumble over my words? Would I make sense? What was my point anyway? And where was my cheat sheet index card?

I was introduced and I smiled as I silently asked the Holy Spirit to use my mouth as a vessel. I knew I wasn't really there to talk about flowers. I was suddenly excited to have the mystery revealed to me, too.

I shared about the Mexican orchids and told funny things that had happened to me as a missionary. The audience was enthusiastic. I shared about moving to a new place where I was a fish out of water. I saw understanding nods. I shared the theme my mother had planted in my brain and the thought that I would somehow bloom no matter where I was. I saw several women smiling and one young woman crying.

Then I started to cry. Just a little cry came out, but no one could miss it. I stopped. I had to get a hold of myself.

"I always do this when I talk about my mother. It's not that she's bad, it's that I miss her so terribly much." That was the wrong thing to say. Another cry came out of my well-trained, experienced mouth. I couldn't believe it. It was against the rules of speech etiquette. Well, this was probably going to be my last speech anyway.

I got a hold of myself and continued. "Her motto lifted me up many times during those first years here." I shared about the tulips we discovered when the snow finally started to melt and how I took it as a sign of hope. A sign that God was with me.

The speech went very well after all. I finished to enthusiastic women on their feet applauding. Maybe my speaking career wasn't over. I sat down and said a hundred prayers of thanksgiving.

Then I felt a tug on my arm.

71

"I needed to hear what you were saying tonight. Thank you so much!" The young woman who earlier had tears in her eyes shared with me about moving here from a metropolitan area a few months earlier to be with her fiance. Although she loved him dearly, she couldn't decide if she would be able to live in such a small, rural community so far from her home. That morning she had told her fiance she would have to think about it. She felt she received her answer from my message of hope.

I hugged her and held her hand. I told her that I was not to be thanked and that I had nothing to do with this. I shared about the change in topic and the strange turn of events. We smiled as we considered that she was probably the reason why.

The Holy Spirit works in mysterious ways. And great and wondrous will those mysteries be to those who are open to them!

Mother Shepherd

---

*"I am the good shepherd. I know my own and my own
know me, just as the Father knows me and I know the
Father." (vv. 14-15)*

Liliana called me to her room at three that afternoon. "Chaplain," she said, "can I bother you to come and give me and my
family communion tomorrow afternoon at two?"

Liliana and I had had a great relationship since she had been
admitted into the hospital five days ago. She had talked endlessly
of her children — all eleven — and their spouses and children.
Two were already widowed and one was divorced. She knew what
all the "grands" and "greats" were up to. Liliana was a proud shepherd of her flock.

She was also very honest about what was happening to her
body and what her future held. She was firm in her faith. Liliana
loved the Lord. "He loves me because he sure hears enough from
me," she would always say. She felt good about her faith.

But she didn't feel good about her present condition. Her di-
alysis sessions didn't go well and she had made a decision to stop
treatments. She had her daughter call the family; they would gather
tomorrow and have communion as a family for the last time.

I was nervous. I wanted it to go just right. I prepared the
elements, prayed, and read a meditation I would share.

The service at Liliana's hospital bed was beautiful. Thirty-
eight of us were crammed into her private room. Tears flowed
freely as Liliana told her children she was so blessed to see that
they had all made it with so many of the "grands" coming also.
My own tears fell as I considered the words of institution.

I looked at Liliana and she smiled at me. "Thank you so much for doing this," she whispered. She winked at me. I continued, choking back tears as I considered Liliana, her family, and the words of holy communion.

We all took communion. We all shared the peace. And we all cried. As I blessed the group, I turned to Liliana and asked her if she had anything to say. She lifted her hand, looked around, and said, "You have all been wonderful to me. I love you so much and you have loved me so much. God will bless you forever for that."

To this day, I cannot preside over communion without recalling the feeling I had giving communion to Liliana and her family. Liliana, the shepherd, had blessed us all by her request, by her faith, and by her words. God, the shepherd of all, was surely present in this place.

See The Little Light Shine

*"Philip asked, 'Do you understand what you are read-
ing?' He replied, 'How can I, unless someone guides
me?'" (vv. 30-31)*

She was so patient. Again and again she would explain things
in different ways until her students would understand. Until she
saw "a little light shine in their eyes," she always said. Mrs. DiCarlo
was the sixth grade teacher and working with children until they
understood a certain point was her job. It was also her joy.

Mrs. DiCarlo brought in lots of materials to illustrate a point.
Figurines, posters, music, science experiments, odd-looking crea-
tures, and a variety of lively examples were paraded endlessly in
her classroom. She made learning fun and interesting. This mod-
est woman used much of her paycheck to buy materials and sup-
plies for the classroom. Her class was fun and exciting and she
was committed to making her point known.

Philip was committed to make Christ known. He was led by
the Holy Spirit to the eunuch in this passage in Acts. The eunuch
was trying to read the message of the prophet Isaiah but did not
understand. When Philip approached him in the chariot, the eunuch cried out, "How can I understand [what I am reading] unless
someone explains it to me?" Philip rode alongside the eunuch
until he understood the meaning of the passage. He had patience
for the eunuch. Philip led the eunuch to understand.

Teachers, professors, child caregivers, and countless others take
great pains to help people understand things. Many teachers still
hold their children's hands; they care deeply about their pupils.
And most have the courage, wisdom, and patience to wait it out
until they "see the little light shine" in their students' eyes.

A Life For A Life

"No one has greater love than this, to lay down one's life for one's friends." (v. 13)

Who would lay down his life for a friend? Many of us have very dear friends: we play with them, we cry with them, and we share time with them. But who can honestly say he would lay down a life for a friend?

On March 31, 1998, four little girls, aged eleven to twelve, said goodbye to their parents that morning. One had just moved to the city of 46,000. One played basketball and volleyball. Another was outgoing and planned to try out for the cheerleading squad. The last was a cheerful, chatty student.

The girls were students at Westside Middle School. Another day of school. Another day of the same routine for 250 students in the sixth and seventh grades.

But during the day the fire alarm sounded. Children usually are never frightened because an alarm is usually a drill. Often the drills are seen as welcome chances to get out of class and chat outside until the teachers give the thumbs up that the students can go back inside. This was also a false alarm. There was no fire.

The children were hurrying outside, obediently filing out of the school to stand along the fence when two classmates, ages eleven and thirteen, opened fire on them. Fellow classmates. Friends.

Ten children were shot and received treatment. The four girls were shot and killed. An English teacher, Shannon Wright, who was only 32 years old, was shot and killed as she jumped in front of her students. She took two bullets. The girl she shielded was unharmed.

The shooters were dressed in camouflage, armed with several weapons. In one carefully orchestrated moment, five lives were snuffed out by two heavily armed classmates. Heavily armed friends.

But many more could have been killed. Mrs. Wright shielded at least one of her homeroom students. It is possible she saved more. She gave her life for those children. Selflessly, she gave her life so others could live.

New Hope

"But you will receive power when the Holy Spirit has come upon you; and you will be my witnesses in Jerusalem, in all Judea and Samaria, and to the ends of the earth." (v. 8)

Chiapas is one of the two poorest states in Mexico. Viewed largely as an embarrassment to the rest of the nation, Chiapas is unsuccessfully trying to deal with hostile tribes, high illiteracy, and very rugged terrain. Travel is difficult through the subtropical and highland forests, and the existence of many language groups makes it difficult to communicate.

Outside the highland city of San Cristobal de las Casas is the village of San Juan Chamula, where the Chamula tribe resides, growing corn and selling firewood for sustenance. Most keep cattle for milk and meat. Extreme violence, domestic abuse, and an oppressive economy make this a village closed to outsiders.

Many years ago, Christian missionaries moved into this area. They were met with much suspicion and hostility by the Chamulas. But the missionaries did nothing other than observe for many years. The villagers watched as the missionaries grew food, raised their young children, and lived outside the Chamula area. Slowly, the missionaries gained the villagers' trust and began to share with them the good news of Jesus Christ.

These outsiders have influenced the group as they shared their faith with the Chamulas. Some tribal members converted from their pagan religion to a modified Christo-pagan religion common in Christian churches in Chiapas. The new converts renounced violence, spoke against domestic abuse, and created co-ops. But many were met with hostility and some suffered violence and even death.

At first, those who renounced the Chamula way of life were ostracized. Their huts were burned, their cattle killed, and their crops destroyed. Some retracted their statements of faith and returned in shame. Some stood fast in their new faith.

Those who survived started a new village on the other side of the town of San Cristobal de las Casas. *Nueva Esperanza*, they called it — "New Hope." New hope that they might be left in peace to worship the same Christ we worship. New hope that their trade cooperatives might be successful enough to sustain them. New hope that their fellow Chamulas might also find peace in knowing Christ.

Our Chamula brothers and sisters received power when the Holy Spirit came upon them and they are able to witness in Chiapas — and to the ends of the earth.

Gift From God

---

*"Now they know that everything you have given me is
from you...." (v. 7)*

Brian could feel the heat of anger rising in his neck. His left
hand curled into a fist and he hit the palm of his right hand. He felt
dizzy as he looked around.

Clothes, towels, and sheets were scattered all over the living
room. A glass of orange juice was empty, the contents still drib-
bling down the side of the coffee table. A towel landed at his feet.
His one-year-old looked up at him and giggled, making Brian even
more angry.

He picked Adam up and set him down hard on the kitchen
table. "It took me an hour to fold all this laundry," he shouted. "I
leave the room for ten minutes and you just make a mess of everything!" Brian could feel blood rush to his head as he reached for
Adam. Adam became quiet.

Brian's hand was poised to strike but it stopped in midair. Adam
had his arms out, saying, "Up, Daddy, up." Brian choked down a
gasp. What was he about to do? Did Brian think he could actually
hit Adam? Was the laundry that important? He cried in shame as
he picked Adam up. He hugged Adam tight and looked at him
long and hard.

Adam was the child they had waited for. Jen and Brian had
tried everything to conceive and finally were approved for adop-
tion. Adam came three years later.

Adam was five days old when the papers were signed. Pure
joy had filled Brian's heart at the sight of the baby. He was so
sweet, so small, so innocent. All four grandparents, several aunts,
uncles, and cousins had been there for Adam's homecoming. Bright

balloons were everywhere. The presents were heaped in the virtual mountain with wrapping paper of light blues.

The baptism was two months later. Brian had held Adam as the pastor began the baptismal service. Brian couldn't seem to let go of Adam as he listened to the words. "In holy baptism our gracious heavenly Father liberates us from sin ... We are born children of a fallen humanity ... In the waters of baptism we are reborn children of God and inheritors of eternal life."

Brian stared as the pastor took little Adam, held him tight, and poured water over his head. "By water and the Holy Spirit we are made members of the church which is the body of Christ. As we live with him and with his people we grow in faith, love, and obedience to the will of God."

The pastor had challenged Jen and Brian in the sermon. Brian recalled the words: "No matter what mischief Adam will get into, he is still God's child, washed clean by the water of his baptism. No matter what Adam does or says, he is still full of the Holy Spirit. For by baptism he has been made perfect in God's sight."

Brian reached for Adam. He cradled Adam in the recliner and together they read books. The laundry would keep. Brian needed time with his perfect little gift from God.

Encouragement

*"When the Spirit of truth comes, he will guide you into
all the truth...." (v. 13)*

Words are important. They start wars, create unions, and touch
our emotions. One man knew the impact of positive words. He
touched others by believing in them so much that they in turn believed in themselves. His name was Joseph.

Joseph was naturally cheerful, encouraging, and generous. He
was also very exuberant about his faith and told everyone he saw
what Jesus meant to him and what he had seen. Joseph used words
to communicate the gospel, to help others understand it and be
supported.

Joseph was an apostle sent to Antioch to help the church grow.
He was a Levite, born in Cyprus. He sold a field he owned and
brought the money to the disciples, giving it to them for their ministry. Joseph sent the disciples on their way with words of support
and affirmation.

The other disciples renamed him Barnabas, "son of encouragement." They felt this name fit him better. Barnabas turned out
to fit his name very well.

When Paul came to Jerusalem after his conversion, most of
the new Christians did not want to associate with Paul. They knew
the reputation he had. He had been a persecutor, an enemy of the
Christian community. But Barnabas wanted Paul to have a chance
to prove himself. What if Paul really was a changed man? What if
Paul really did love the Lord as he said? Barnabas wanted Paul to
have the opportunity of ministry.

Barnabas and Paul went on a missionary journey together, taking Mark with them. Mark was Barnabas' younger cousin. Mark

turned back after their arrival in Perga, much to Barnabas' and Paul's regret.

Barnabas and Paul continued their missionary work. When they set out for a second journey, Barnabas once again sought out Mark, but Paul was against it. Paul felt that Mark was undependable. Barnabas wanted to give Mark a chance, as he had given Paul a chance.

Barnabas went with Mark on a missionary journey, while Paul took Silas with him. Mark responded to Barnabas' encouragement. Paul later wrote several times in his epistles that Mark had proven to be a valuable assistant. It helped that Barnabas had taken Mark to familiar territory, to Cyprus, where Mark had worked before. Mark was welcome there and he witnessed the results of the work he had done two years earlier.

We don't read much about Barnabas after his second missionary trip. He stayed in Cyprus, his home, where he had a flourishing ministry which was carried to North Africa.

Throughout the Bible we read of Paul's stubbornness. But we also see how stubborn Barnabas was. Barnabas believed in others and would not let them miss their potential. Barnabas overlooked others' faults and encouraged them with care and compassion.

Barnabas did not seek his own glory; he was a faithful servant who wanted what was best for the Church. He gave generously of his life and material goods for the relief of the poor and for the disciples' ministry. He was instrumental in spreading the gospel by encouraging both Mark and Paul in their missionary work.

Lesson From The Shamrock

"For all who are led by the Spirit of God are children of God." (v. 14)

Shar was worried. She was in charge of the children's sermon this Sunday. And it was Holy Trinity Sunday! She had read for weeks about the meaning of Trinity Sunday and had learned much from it. But which image would speak to the little ones who would come forward?

She considered the classic example of the apple cut in half. Shar had seen it in a children's sermon book. She could show that although the apple had three parts, skin, fruit, and seed, it was still called an apple.

Or was the illustration of the newborn more apt to catch their attention? The baby is brother, son, and grandson all in one, yet still named John. Shar wondered about what she would say. Maybe the apple illustration would be better. It was Saturday evening and she was growing more nervous.

Her mind wandered to the past week. Shar was a third grade teacher at the elementary school downtown. She loved to see the eager young learners as they studied different things. This month was Irish month and the children heard Irish music, watched Irish dancing, saw the beautiful countryside, learned about the terrible wars, and ate Irish food. They had great fun. The students even tried to speak English with an Irish brogue.

Though it wasn't March, Shar included a study on Saint Patrick, the man who was sold at age sixteen to be a laborer only later to become the patron saint of Ireland. When Patrick escaped from his slavery, he became a monk. One of the objects he used as he taught the concept of the Holy Trinity was the shamrock.

That's it! Shar would use a shamrock, with its three leaves, to illustrate the Trinity. She could explain how the shamrock had three even sides, yet each part was important. Each side represented a part of the Trinity: the Father, Son, and Holy Spirit. Each side was a mystery to understand, but each side represented a powerful part of the Christian faith. As the shamrock's leaves protect the ground underneath, so God protects us with the three parts of the Trinity.

Relief flooded her as Shar prepared her talk. She gathered up several shamrocks from the garlands left over from class. She would have enough for each child to take one home. It would be a fun little reminder of the children's sermon. Shar was getting excited. And in her excitement, the little poem her mother used to say every morning when Shar went off to school repeated in her head:

The sacred Three
Be over me;
The blessing of
The Trinity.

Corpus Christi
Mark 14:12-16, 22-26

The Body Of Christ ... For You

*"While they were eating, he took a loaf of bread,
and after blessing it he broke it and gave it to them...."*
(v. 22)

"This is the body of Christ, broken for you."

"The body of Christ, broken for you."

Sammy's head pounded as she repeated the words over and over again for the people as they came up for the sacrament of Holy Communion.

"The body of Christ, broken for you. The body of Christ, broken for you ..."

Yeah, she thought. My body is broken. It's so large, I can barely stand up this long. I have no energy, no strength, no stamina.

"The body of Christ, broken for you." Sammy had been asked to be a Eucharistic minister soon after the new priest came to their parish. She loved the new priest instantly. He had the kind eyes of her grandfather. He had the wit of her brother. He had the patience of a saint. And he didn't look directly at her enormous body when Sammy spoke to him.

Father Jerry didn't mind listening to her fears of being in front of people. He told her to think about his request and get back to him. Sammy had agonized over the decision. She would love to be a Eucharistic minister, to help Father Jerry. To help with such an important ritual was a supreme honor for her. But to be in front of people was too difficult. It would be too embarrassing.

Father Jerry wouldn't take no for an answer. "I'd still like you to help me at the nursing home, Samantha — and at the camp for children with disabilities during the summer. We'll do it together. You'll be fine. You'll see."

Sure! He had probably given communion a million times. And at sixty, he had a nice figure. He undoubtedly always had.

But she couldn't disappoint him, so every Friday Sammy would meet him at the nursing home. She was nervous the first time. She could feel her heart beat in her hands as she carefully lifted the host from the paten and put it into the people's hands. She didn't want to crush the light wafers. They seemed so fragile.

She was feeling a lot better about helping at communion. The old people didn't seem to notice her size. She still sweat a little, but she didn't shake nearly as badly.

Summer camp time came and she agreed to help. Little children snickered at her when they first saw her, but they got over it. It was so nice to walk in the woods after church! It gave Sammy such a peaceful feeling.

"The body of Christ, broken for you." If that line of people didn't go down, Sammy swore she was going to faint. A man walked up, hunched over with age. He stood tall with great effort and took the host. He looked her straight in the eye and said, "Thank you," in a whisper. He slowly bent over again and gingerly walked away. She turned to look at him.

She gave wafer after wafer. A little girl was pushed forward in her wheelchair. She had beautiful eyes and drooled. She was such a cutie. Sammy gave her a wafer and was rewarded with a smile. Sammy's eyes watered.

Why was she feeling sorry for herself when some people had a right to complain about their bodies? They didn't seem to be whining about their body condition. Could she?

"The body of Christ, broken for you." Broken for Sammy. Broken by being whipped. Broken by humiliation. Broken by death on a cross.

Sammy could feel her head pounding, but her heart seemed to be singing. Christ's body was broken for Sammy. For all believers. Not just for pretty people. Not just for those without disability. Not just for the courageous.

Sammy smiled as she took another wafer. "The body of Christ, broken for you." This time she smiled as she said it.

Keeping The Sabbath

"The sabbath was made for humankind, and not humankind for the sabbath...." (v. 27)

Take a day to nourish your soul. Keeping the Sabbath isn't about rules and restrictions. It's about setting aside a day each week for the soulful activities that our high-pressure careers and weekday responsibilities squeeze out.*

Connie's mother wouldn't hear of it. "We don't shop on Sunday. We don't wash our hair, we don't work, we don't buy. You've heard this your whole life, Connie. Why would you think anything is different?"

Connie was frustrated. Her friends were going to the mall to buy CDs, and Connie was delighted when they called to ask if she could be ready in ten minutes. She enthusiastically cried, "Yes." But her enthusiasm turned to gloom when her mother gave her stern answer. Connie wondered: was she the only one who felt this way?

Bob loved summer Sundays. They were times when his family went camping. They would pack up the camper on Thursday evening, and as soon as Mom and Dad came home from work on Friday, they would be off on a new adventure. They tried to stay within six hours from their hometown and they explored every corner of their state and beyond. They lived for the weekends.

When Bob and Connie were married several years later, they didn't think their views of Sunday would conflict. Connie loved to camp and Bob enjoyed all the home-cooked meals Connie made. But they couldn't agree on their Sunday routine. Connie needed to go to church; Bob felt it was his only chance to get away from a pressured week.

They needed to find a happy middle ground for both of them. They are extreme examples coming together, but they found a common ground: camping twice a month and attending church twice a month. Bob and Connie were able to relax after their decision. Although they made concessions when special things came up, they realized that Sundays for them were times to do things they loved and to focus on the beauty of nature, the wondrous gifts of God, and the strong relationship they were creating.

*(Information taken from "10 Keys for life: A fresh, life-giving look at the commandments" by Leonard Felder in the March 1997 issue of *The Lutheran* magazine.)

Sharing And Caring

"But just as we have the same spirit of faith that is in accordance with scripture ... we also believe, and so we speak." (v. 13)

Henry hated Arnold. Arnold was always bossing everyone around, arguing, and pointing his little finger when giving orders. Henry was so fed up with it he thought he'd choke Arnold.

Such were Henry's thoughts as he climbed the steps of the church. Hardly a Christian attitude, he thought. Hardly worthy of Christ's love. Henry had thought so long and hard about all of Arnold's faults, he could rattle them off without hesitation. And often he did to his wife, Kitty. But Kitty would just smile and return to her work after Henry's tirade.

Henry didn't dare share his thoughts with anyone in the church. Arnold was a fourth generation member, a member of council, past president of every committee, and a faithful Sunday school teacher, even at 79. Henry would be laughed at, he was sure, if he voiced his complaints to anyone.

The church bells rang and Henry felt his heart pound at the surprisingly loud sound they made. He was so startled he sat for a moment at the top step. No one was around to see him and he leaned his back against the cool rail. He hoped Kitty was having a nice time at the conference, but he was eager to have her back. He always missed her when she was gone. He stared out at the field across the street. The sun was bright in the sky.

Henry was only a first generation member here. He had moved here for a job and met Kitty. They were married shortly after and now it was already thirty years ago. Time seemed to have flown by as they watched their three children become parents themselves.

The "grands" were all little and Henry couldn't wait to see them every spring and fall. He could never get enough of them when they were together.

It felt good to sit for a while. Henry supposed he was missing the announcements, but that wasn't important. It was nice to feel the sun on his face and feel the coolness of the rail. His mind wandered to the countless events that had taken place at this church: their wedding; the children's baptisms, confirmations, recitals, plays, their weddings; and finally the grandchildren's baptisms. He loved this church and he was proud of it.

Lost in thought, Henry didn't even notice that Arnold was sitting quietly next to him. "You looked so peaceful, I thought I better catch some of that spirit from you, Henry. Do you mind if I sit with you for a while?" What could Henry say? These weren't his steps!

Arnold was in a chatty mood. He shared with Henry all the church meant to him. He asked if Henry even knew they had thirteen grandchildren and five great-grandchildren. So many to keep track of, Arnold said!

Arnold told Henry of the countless events that had happened at this church: his wedding to his late wife 54 years ago, their children's baptisms, confirmations, church plays, potlucks, and celebrations. Arnold became silent as he considered all the things that had taken place here.

"I get a little protective of this place, you know. I'm just so worried that people won't love it enough. It's silly, but I want this church to be loved way after my great-grandchildren are gone. It's meant so much to me. Can you understand that?"

Henry continued to stare out at the horizon. He understood. He had had those same thoughts sitting there. Henry smiled at Arnold. "If we go in now, do you think we'll still be able to catch the sermon?" They smiled as they got up and entered the church together.

Proper 6
2 Corinthians 5:6-10 (11-13) 14-17

Made In The Image Of God

> *"From now on, therefore, we regard no one from a human point of view; even though we once knew Christ from a human point of view, we know him no longer in that way. So if anyone is in Christ, there is a new creation: everything old has passed away; see, everything has become new!" (vv. 16-17)*

Darla had always suffered from bouts of depression and low self-esteem. As a teenager, she felt as if everyone stared at her whenever she would get another pimple. Though thin, Darla was sure all the kids at school would notice if she gained a pound. Darla felt she was the only one on earth who had to suffer a combination of large nose, fine hair, tiny ears, and crooked teeth. She hated herself.

Many years of counseling had helped her gain perspective. After all, didn't every person have flaws? The counselor told her *everyone* had insecurities and imperfections, but how we handled these feelings made the difference.

Darla recalled the four happiest days of her life: her wedding and the birth of each of the three girls. She had taken down all the mirrors in the house and prayed the girls would inherit their looks from their father. Time went on and a mirror was added every now and then.

Darla and her husband went to a party one night and met nice people from their new neighborhood. Darla kept wondering what people thought of her. Would they notice the scar under her chin? What was her hair doing? Would they think the mole on her neck was a pimple? She went to the bathroom and looked in the mirror.

She tugged at her hair, covered the mole, and checked the scar. She was fine, she reminded herself. Just then she caught sight of a sticker on the corner of the mirror. The inscription made her pause: "Do you see yourself as God sees you?" It had the name of the local Catholic diocese at the bottom. She read the question again. Do you see yourself as God sees you?

Darla stopped fidgeting with her face and wondered. How *did* God see her? Did God see the problems on her face? On her body? In her mind? Did God see the obstacles, faults, character flaws that every one of us has?

She practiced her self-esteem mental exercise. What was the positive alternative? Made in the image of God? Surely God wasn't that ugly! She caught herself. Made in God's likeness — with feelings, thoughts, and fears?

The question from the silver sticker stuck by her for months as she pondered the answer. Did she have the potential to be a child of God? Finally, she reached a conclusion: "I, Darla, with all my skills and scars, am one of God's children. A child of God made to love and care for others. I am made in the image of God."

Today, there is a small piece of paper on Darla's bathroom mirror. Daily she asks herself, with a smile: "Do you see yourself as God sees you?" She always nods yes.

Calming The Storm

"He woke up and rebuked the wind, and said to the sea, 'Peace! Be still!' " (v. 39)

The Lake of Galilee is on the northern end of the rift valley. It is the world's lowest (680 feet below sea level) freshwater lake. It is about 150 feet at its deepest. The lake covers about ninety square miles.

In Jesus' time the lake was a rich fishing place. Several villages were built around the lake and it was important for the local economy. It was also important for Jesus' disciples, as Jesus chose seven of his followers from the lake.

To this day two varieties of fish are caught in the lake: tilapia and sardines. They are caught by modern methods now, but in Jesus' day they were caught with nets. The nets were circular with small weights spaced around the perimeter. As the net was thrown in a spinning motion on the water, the weights dragged the net down and the fisherman would pull the cord attached at the center. The fish would become entangled and be covered by the net, making it easy for the fish to be hauled to shore or to the boat.

The lake and its fishing symbols were important to Jesus' ministry. He used fishing, water, and catching terms because he knew his audience would understand. Using terminology that helps paint a picture is important: using terminology that is familiar to the audience will make their lives connect to the story.

Once Jesus calmed a great storm. The Lake of Galilee often saw sudden storms, and the fishermen knew the fury a storm could hold. They were fearful. Jesus calmed not only their fears but also the storm.

Are you facing a storm: Are you in the midst of a raging fury? Are you stifled by a crisis that you can't see past?

Let Jesus' love unfold you like a net. Let God's strong arms pull you in so you can live the life God intends for you. Ask God to help you. God has created life in you. Don't allow it to be destroyed.

Proper 8
Mark 5:21-43

How We Are God's Tea Cups

"Daughter, your faith has made you well; go in peace...." (v. 34)

The tea cup was stained. It was Mary's favorite cup, with flowers and leaves hand-painted on the outside. Gold leafing trimmed the rim. And the handle was curved very delicately. But the inside was stained from tea.

Mary set to soaking it in a bit of bleach. Her thoughts turned to the first communion class that she had to teach this Sunday. She had been trying to find a way to explain the meaning behind communion and the ritual that went with it. She breathed a quick prayer for help.

As she washed and dried her beloved tea cup, Mary found the answer. She would use her tea cup! She would explain that just like her tea cup is precious to Mary, we are precious to God, more precious than gold. God loves us as no one can. But just like the tea cup becomes stained, we make mistakes. We gossip, we tell lies, we covet things, and we sin. We become stained. But Jesus, in his death, became the bleach we need to renew our lives so that we can once again shine with God's love. As we are cleaned and dried, we are reminded to try again, to love one another, and be true to Jesus' example.

Mary found a box to put her tea cup in. Very carefully, she wrapped it in tissue paper and sealed the box. She got a warm feeling all over as she imagined that God, who loves us so much, wraps us in his arms and looks at us like a treasure. Mary breathed a word of thanks and continued on her day.

Blessed To Be A Blessing

"Therefore I am content with weaknesses, insults, hardships, persecutions, and calamities for the sake of Christ; for whenever I am weak, then I am strong."
(v. 10)

Mark had loved helping out ever since he was young. When he was a teenager, his favorite activities were mowing the church lawn and assisting in the liturgy. Mowing was the best because he could take the lawn tractor out and make designs in the grass, make circles and figure-eights on the freshly cut lawn and nobody knew the difference. "His" lawn — all twelve acres — was his pride.

And assisting the pastor was fun for him. Mark loved singing the liturgy and reading the lessons. He was not ashamed to admit he liked the sound of his voice over the sound system. He enjoyed the looks on people's faces as he bent over and gave them the communion wine. To him it was a privilege.

Mark went to seminary and returned to his hometown whenever he could. The town was only two thousand strong, and he knew everyone and everyone's business. And they knew his. Mark's life was uncomplicated. He married his high school sweetheart; they had four children and two dogs. He loved being a pastor for two small churches and enjoyed being with the people.

When Mark became ill, he wasn't worried. He probably had eaten something that disagreed with him. But three months and fourteen tests later, the news was not good: cancer was in his abdomen and the prognosis was not promising. But Mark insisted he was not to be pitied. He underwent chemotherapy and his intern preached and visited more often, but Mark still made it to the office every day. Mark read books about bald jokes. He wrote in his journal daily. He wrote his children letters and made the most of every day.

Mark led his children to count their blessings every night before they fell asleep. He reminded them how fragile yet wonderful life is. Mark knew he was blessed. He knew God loved him through and through.

Mark died when he was just about to turn 45. His wife and children were at his side. He was sad to know he would not see them grow up, but he was happy to have had this time with them. It was hard to make them understand that while they would miss him, Mark would be in heaven.

Mark was blessed in his short life. He offered all he had to his family and friends. He was a blessing to those who knew him. He was a blessing because he had been blessed.

Dance Of Gratitude

"David and all the house of Israel were dancing before the Lord with all their might...." (v. 5)

Anna dances. Ever since she was cured of a childhood disease, she has danced. She dances out of gratitude. Her motions are a song of thanksgiving.

Her body moves to the music, making liturgy come alive. Tiny feet arch and point. Long legs carry her across the floor as she arches and twirls. Her torso twists and bends effortlessly. Her arms extend elegantly. Even her long hair has a rhythm all its own. She makes the words and music one with her body.

Anna dances in church. She praises God and rejoices with beautiful moves, setting the words to music. Many have heard the words before, but set to dance they seem to take on new meaning.

Her body crouches low, slowly rising. Her hands reach upward as she looks up. The music continues and Anna sways gracefully. Her legs bend and lift her. Her arms fold tightly around herself. Anna looks upward as if crying out. Anguish fills her face.

Anna spins slowly and moves about faster, twirling and bending. "Glory to the Father, and to the Son, and to the Holy Spirit; as it was in the beginning, is now, and will be forever." She pauses and arches ever so slowly, then points to heaven.

Quietly, she bows. Quietly, our hearts are touched. Anna praises God with her body, and we rejoice.

Proper 11
Mark 6:30-34, 53-56

Bartolomé de las Casas, Missionary

"As he went ashore, he saw a great crowd; and he had compassion for them, because they were like sheep without a shepherd; and he began to teach them many things." (v. 34)

Professor Bob Corbett celebrates and laments the work of Bartolomé de las Casas. The following is paraphrased from Professor Corbett's biography of Bishop de las Casas.

Bartolomé de las Casas was born in Seville, Spain, in 1474. His father sailed with Columbus in 1492. De las Casas became a priest at the age of 36 and Bartolomé himself made the third voyage with Columbus as a Dominican priest to the New World. He settled into his new surroundings.

It is said that he was deeply moved by the harsh treatment of slaves, so he gave up his slaves. When he saw the brutality the indigenous people had to endure at the hands of the Spanish explorers, Bartolomé spoke out. He told people of the Indians' plight. He exposed the hardship they had to endure. He became their champion.

Father Bartolomé worked throughout the Caribbean Islands and Central America to end slavery for the native population. He worked hard to stop the horrible treatment women received at the hands of the military. But he didn't do it by speaking out against slavery. He demanded instead peaceful treatment of the Amerindians. He even persuaded the King of Spain to make new laws toward more humane treatment of the indigenous people, but the laws were ignored in the New World.

Father de las Casas saw the fragile state of the Arawak Indians in Hispañola. They could not tolerate the heavy work and hard labor expected of them by the Spaniards. Unfortunately, de las

Casas suggested that black slaves be imported to do the heavy work. Father de las Casas felt that the African slaves were "constitutionally more fit for hard labor than were the Amerindians." Black slavery in the New World had begun.

But Father Bartolomé de las Casas had good intentions and good will. He did not have the foresight to see his mistake and he put heart over head in his concern for his neighbors, the Amerindians. He always insisted that the Amerindians were made in the image of God and should not to be treated as animals.

In 1516, Bartolomé de las Casas was celebrated as the official protector of the Indians, and the following year he negotiated land in Venezuela for an experiment in evangelization. The experiment failed. He returned to Spain and then again to Mexico where de las Casas became bishop of Chiapas, the southernmost state of Mexico, and Cuba in 1543. This was 41 years after coming to the New World.

He finally returned to Spain in 1547 where he continued the debate over the maltreatment of the Amerindians. Bishop de las Casas called those who supported Indian slavery "misguided" and given up to evil by God. De las Casas wrote, "Are we not obliged to love them as ourselves?" But those who had never been outside of Spain felt these writings were romantic, exotic, and fictional. They were not taken seriously there. Bishop de las Casas died in 1566.

Proper 12
John 6:1-21

Miracles

---

*"So they gathered them up, and from the fragments of
the five barley loaves, left by those who had eaten, they
filled twelve baskets." (v. 13)*

Some people have spent countless hours trying to explain how
Jesus could possibly have fed 5,000 men, their wives, and their
children — possibly 25,000 people! — with only two fish and five
loaves of bread. Some have used physics calculations. Some have
used the theory of good-neighborliness as each person shared what
he had. Some people feel it is not possible or true. What do you
believe?

In our Christian faith, we read about things that we cannot
possibly understand. People have argued that the Sea of Reeds,
which Moses passed through, was actually a trickle of water in the
sand. Some people regularly discount miracles in the Bible because
they are not explainable in everyday terms. They are mysteries.

Oh, but is it so bad to have mysteries? God's power can accomplish more than we can possibly imagine. God does not mind
if we appreciate miracles without trying to figure out the mechan-
ics or possibilities. Some things are too awesome to explain away.

Consider one modern-day miracle. How could a body that was
made to carry one, possibly two babies, carry seven? The
McCaughey septuplets made history when they were born in Iowa
on November 19, 1997. Bobbi and Kenneth McCaughey, who had
an infant daughter, became parents again that day — seven times
over — surrounded by controversy and anger, celebration and joy.
America's first living septuplets are not only living, but also they
made it to their first birthday healthy and will be with us many,
many years to come.

Barring any conversations of ethics, can the birth of the McCaugheys be considered a miracle? It's not easily explained. The septuplets' doctors both say it was a miracle. And is it so bad for our faith journey to consider miracles in our world today?

Consider miracles for what they are: God's signs of unlimited power beyond our imagination or rationale. Mysteries to behold and strengthen our faith. Thank God that miracles still happen!

Trickle Up

"But each of us was given grace according to the measure of Christ's gift." (v. 7)

Paul calls for unity and gives us the seven signs of Christian unity as we make up the body of Christ: one Lord, one faith, one baptism, one spirit, one hope, one God, one body. Together they make up the parts of the body of Christ. And to each one of us who believe in Christ was given a certain talent, a gift, to be used for the good of the body of Christ, for the good of others.

Mildred Leet used her talent for the good of others. Mrs. Leet gives "seed money" to people to start businesses and be productive in their labor. She and her husband, Glen Leet, started giving grants through their foundation called Trickle Up.

One woman in Barbados used Trickle Up's money for a thriving jam business. One woman used the grant to start a hat business. One man's idea of turning old Christmas trees into walking sticks flourished with his seed money. He sells his sticks at $40 each and has sold more than 300! Some people use their money for materials such as sewing machines or gardening supplies.

Over 70,000 grants have been approved and distributed in fifty countries with 350,000 people being trained in businesses. In a recent interview with Alex Tresniowski and Bob Meadows for *People* magazine, Mrs. Leet explained that "a little bit of help can make all the difference."

By giving $700 and asking for a promise that twenty percent of the profits be reinvested into the business, Mrs. Leet gives people the chance to be productive. Her daughter says her mother feels that the world is a village where people are improved one person at a time.

One Lord, one faith, one baptism, one spirit, one hope, one God, one body. The ordinary person isn't expected to do exactly what Mrs. Leet has done. But what if we did all we could for the betterment of others? One person can make a big difference.

(Based on an article in *People* magazine, 1/11/99.)

A Change Of Heart

---

*"Therefore be imitators of God, as beloved children,
and live in love, as Christ loved us...." (vv. 1-2)*

Moe wasn't always so nice. He used to be a shrewd business-man, calculating profit in every business move. He didn't care that his developments tore down long-standing neighborhoods. He didn't care that new tenants paid three times more than what they used to. He wanted money, power, and status. Moe wanted it all.

Moe didn't believe in religion, but his business manager had convinced him that making contributions to strategic charities and organizations would increase his status in the small community. "You don't have to do anything, just give," he was told. And give he did. One million dollars to a service organization and one million dollars to a church recovering from a fire. Done. He didn't have to think about it anymore.

Until Paula stood on his doorstep. Paula was a young businesswoman in the community and a member of the church where Moe had donated so much. Moe's manager allowed her to come in. This wouldn't take long.

Paula got right to the point. What had convinced him to give to their church? Why that church and not another one that was suffering from flood damage? Was this money from a legitimate source? What did he gain from it?

Moe smiled. Paula was a lot like Moe's younger brother, so trusting, so innocently asking for the truth. But there was something about Paula's manner that wouldn't allow Moe to brush her off so easily. He invited her to stay for lunch.

Over shrimp cocktails, Moe explained that, off the record, he had been attracted to the church because it was downtown, had the most exposure, and would give him in turn the most coverage for his donation. It made him feel good to be able to give such a big amount. It would give him more status in the community.

Paula stared at him. She didn't understand. Moe tried to let her see his side of life. Money, power, control, prestige. That was important in his life. Wasn't that simple enough?

After that long lunch and several meetings, Paula and Moe became fast friends. With her gentle manner, she was able to persuade Moe to come and see the rebuilding progress. With her kindness, she was able to ask Moe what his future intentions were with his money, power, and prestige.

Their friendship deepened and Moe was best man in Paula's wedding. He attended her son's baptism. Soon it was time for the dedication of the building. The pastor came to visit and asked Moe point-blank if he would share his testimony from the pulpit.

Testimony? Moe wondered what that meant for him. The story about the acquisition of all his money? The story of developing large portions of town? "No," the pastor said. "We want to know how you have been changed since you have come to know Christ." Moe was confused. "You don't understand," he said. "I don't know Christ."

"Oh, you will. You'll come to that point pretty soon. I'm sure of it." The pastor sounded so convinced. He left Moe and reminded him that he was due to speak two Sundays from now. Pastor handed Moe a copy of the New Testament to read. "This can be your starting point if you feel the need to do some research for your talk."

Moe looked at the Bible with sticky notes poking out. He was intrigued. He took it upstairs with him. He could spare some time before he turned in for the night. He'd start with the sticky notes.

John 3:16; Matthew 18:20; various Psalms; Jeremiah 29:11. Text after text spoke to Moe. Could it be that the book was speaking to him directly? He wondered as he turned off the light. But he couldn't sleep and he soon turned on the light again and continued reading.

Passage after marked passage caught his attention. He read it like stories, but something was not right. What did this mean to him? How did this apply to his life now? He felt his heart change.

That night was the beginning of Moe's faith life. He visited with the pastor several times and turned his life to Christ. When it came time to give his testimony, it included the knowledge that although he still wanted material things, Moe's life had taken on a new twist. He still wanted money, but this time it would be to give to worthy causes. A new tenement housing project would house the people displaced by his development projects. A new gymnasium in town would help the children have a place to go after school. The flooded church just outside of town could use a new fellowship hall.

He had changed. Moe had felt a call to do something for the good of others. He had felt something deep down in his soul. And he was going to do something about it!

Proper 15
Ephesians 5:15-20

The Invitation To Join

"Be careful then how you live ... understand what the will of the Lord is." (vv. 15, 17)

Pao felt disconnected. Like he didn't belong. Like he didn't have a purpose. He had been struggling with his faith for a while and stopped going to church. He just couldn't bear the questions he had. The words he heard in church didn't make sense.

The pastor came to visit early one morning. It was a Saturday and Pao was on his way to wash the car. The pastor suggested they wash the car together in the driveway. Pastor asked how things were with Pao's wife and children, his job at the bank, and the weather. They lathered up the car.

There was an undercurrent of tension. Pao knew Pastor would ask why he hadn't been in church for several months. He was almost holding his breath. How should he answer Pastor? What was the real answer? Pao rinsed the car.

The car was shining as they worked in silence, each drying a side with circular motions. Birds were chirping in the trees and children were playing across the street. It was a peaceful moment. Pao was waiting for the question.

But the question never came. The car gleamed and Pastor laughed and jokingly suggested maybe next week they do Pastor's car. Pastor looked at his watch and mentioned he had to get some groceries. He thanked Pao for the "good workout" and told him to greet his wife and children. They parted with a warm handshake.

Pao stood in the driveway in silence as Pastor drove off, still holding an old towel. Pastor hadn't said anything about his absence in church. Did he even notice? Didn't Pastor want to know why Pao wasn't coming to church?

Pao thought about it the entire afternoon, wondering what he should say if Pastor came again next week and asked him to explain his absence. Pao just couldn't come up with an answer. It was as if church meant nothing to him other than words. It was as if Pao was watching the service through a tunnel.

Pastor did come the following week and this time he and Pao sat and chatted on the front porch. Pastor asked Pao if he could share something with Pao that happened to him when he was going to school.

Pastor had been away from home at college and didn't have time for church. He avoided going to his parents' home on Sundays, hoping his mother wouldn't invite him to church. She never did. But she did share her excitement about a particular Sunday school lesson she had taught to the children. She'd tell him about a speaker or workshop she had attended. Or she would share about a Bible study she had gone to.

Pastor recalled how excited she always was when she would talk about church. But Pastor didn't feel that way. He felt empty when he would sit in the back of the church, straining to see the minister preach, or the guest speaker speak.

Pastor became acquainted with a Christian woman at college who flatly announced that if he were serious about his intentions, he would have to go to church with her. Every Sunday. She loved church and it was through her excitement that Pastor went with her.

The preacher would engage the congregation, asking them questions and expecting an answer. Wow! Pastor had never seen that before. But the change of heart came one Sunday morning when that minister shared what a privilege it was to be a pastor, to be a part of a unit that was spread throughout the world. "We are one body, we share one God, we share all of life together."

At communion that morning, the minister introduced the elements with, "We share in the life and death of Jesus Christ and God the Father through the sacrament of communion, and because of that, we have communion with all of life. If we want to share in Christ's ministry we must become one with him and identify with him."

110

Those words hit Pastor like nothing else. Suddenly it was clear to him. He could be a part of a church that was connected to the whole Church, a worldwide community of believers, if only he would believe in Christ and be in communion with him. It was profound for him. It changed the way he looked at worship and church.

Pastor looked at Pao. "I recognize your look. You look just like I did twenty years ago. I want you to know that I have been praying for you and want you to know that you don't have to come back to church until you are ready. But when you do, I want you to acknowledge that you are a child of God, part of a larger kingdom, part of all Christendom."

Pastor left soon after but Pao thought about those words throughout the next week. And the next. And the following week he went to church and listened. It took several years for Pao's questions to be answered. He and Pastor talked several times. But the greatest honor for Pao was when Pastor asked Pao to be communion assistant. He felt Pao knew better than anyone what holy communion entailed.

Proper 16
John 6:56-69

Joined Together

"We have come to believe and know that you are the
Holy One of God." (v. 69)

I was nervous. I was asked just a few hours ago to fill in at the nursing home and lead worship. I had never been there, but I lead worship at several other retirement and nursing homes. I wanted to do well.

I prayed as I hung up the phone. Yes, I would be happy to do it. Or maybe I should have been more honest and said I would do it and be happy when it was over. I went over the service and on to other things.

The home was beautifully decorated, the lobby resembling an elegant hotel lobby. Fresh flowers as well as silk arrangements made for a cozy atmosphere. Several people were clustered in groups throughout the lobby, some playing cards, others visiting with each other.

I found my way to a small chapel with new furnishings. The piano was ebony, the chairs matched the plush carpeting, and the hymnbooks had recently been purchased as a gift. The altar was stark, naked, and white, as if it were out of place in its attractive surroundings.

I laid out the elements, rehearsed my reflection, and prayed for calm. A peace came over me as I asked the Holy Spirit's presence in this special place. I stood up and opened the door.

They came in little groups. Fifty men and women came walking, strolling behind a walker, or wheeled in their chairs. They were pleasant and the worship started. I felt very comfortable.

In the middle of my reflection, I noticed one man asleep while several others looked interested. I appreciated both. We sang another song and I spoke the words of instruction. "As often as we eat of this bread and drink from this cup, we proclaim the Lord's death until he comes."

One by one, I went to where they were sitting and gave them the wafer that was dipped in the wine. "This is the body of Christ, broken and given for you. This is the blood of Christ, shed for you." One by one, they opened their mouths and let me put the wafers on their tongues. One by one, each a child of God, each a precious part of the kingdom of God.

It was a holy moment. A sacred truth had been revealed to me in that beautiful, small chapel in the nursing home. One by one, as frail or strong, as young or old, through communion, we are joined together. We left the service filled with hope, filled with the power of Christ's endless love. Filled with the power of his endless life.

Proper 17
Mark 7:1-8, 14-15, 21-23

God Noticed Their Hearts

"So the Pharisees and the scribes asked him, 'Why do your disciples not live according to the traditions of the elders...?' " (v. 5)

The vote to have a new church pictorial directory made was approved. Everyone was excited. The sanctuary had new carpeting, a new banner would be made, and flowerbeds were planted.

A photographer was hired to take pictures of the grounds. The bell tower would be photographed in the morning and at night. The eight-foot steel logo on the outside was polished. The newly seeded lawns were mown. There was excitement in the air. All was readied.

The chairwoman of the pictorial directory had meticulously outlined the calling tree and everyone had a specific appointment time. Anyone late would have to make up the appointment time in a week. She wanted to make sure that everything ran smoothly. Connie didn't like tardiness. And she despised disorderliness. Especially in the church.

Connie was proud of her accomplishments in the church. She was the head of many committees and, at 84, felt she had contributed much to this church. Her parents had come to this church when they were first married, several years before Connie and her five brothers were born. They were all baptized, confirmed, and married here. It was their home church.

The first family came for their pictures. They were dressed in red, the father wearing a red tie with his navy suit and the mother and daughter having matching red dresses. Connie was proud of them.

The next couple came and Connie had them sit in the appointed waiting area. They looked attractive in their elegant clothing. Connie remarked that their picture was sure to come out beautifully.

On and on the members came. Many singles, many couples, and many families. Even a pair of sisters. Much of the day was spent straightening ties, arranging stray hairs, and holding up a hand-held mirror. Connie was happy people were arriving on time. She liked efficiency.

Then a family walked in dressed in denim shirts and jeans. Connie was stunned. She didn't recognize them. Is that what they would wear for the directory? She marched straight toward them just before they entered the waiting area. "Would you rather be photographed tomorrow? If you are on your way somewhere, maybe you would like to come back. I have one opening left tomorrow night at six o'clock. We'll just see you then."

The family was very quiet and left. Connie forgot all about them. The next day went the same as the first. Singles, couples, and families were photographed. Then at six o'clock, the family returned — wearing denim shirts.

Connie couldn't believe it. Didn't they get the hint? They couldn't have meant to be photographed actually wearing farm clothes, could they? She would get to the bottom of this at once.

The gift of grace was not always evident with Connie. She walked up to the mother and asked if they were expecting to be photographed tonight. And in those clothes? What was happening today, she thought? Didn't anyone have respect anymore?

No, Connie was not having any part of this. She measured the candles every Sunday. Exactly twelve to fourteen inches and no more or no less. And the offering plates were placed on the altar exactly six inches to the left of the candle. And the paschal candle was one footstep from the altar. It had to be perfect. This was God's house. This was sacred territory for her. She wasn't going to let anyone spoil this place.

The mother was finally about to answer Connie when the pastor arrived. Pastor was so excited. Had Connie met the new members? They had just moved in two months ago and already were involved in the church. Mother was teaching adult Bible study and Dad was sponsoring the upcoming youth trip. Pastor was very enthusiastic about this family. Didn't Pastor notice their clothes, Connie wondered.

115

Pastor smoothed the moment over and welcomed the family. The pictorial directory turned out beautifully, with people dressed in their best, in their comfortable, and in everything in between. Connie noticed their clothes. Fortunately, God noticed their hearts.

A Different Hunger

---

*"... but a woman whose little daughter had an unclean
spirit immediately heard about him, and she came and
bowed down at his feet." (v. 25)*

Marsha and Richard had a beautiful home on a wooded lot just outside the suburbs. They worked hard to keep it to their standards and they entertained often. A large staff maintained the grounds and the house. Everything ran quite smoothly.

Marsha was a director of a hospice agency; Richard was the president of a prestigious bank. They had a comfortable life although they didn't spend much time in their home. They preferred to be on the go.

Vacations were usually trips to the Cayman Islands, the French Riviera, or Spain. Richard loved the nightlife in Acapulco and the deep-sea fishing in Hawaii. But Marsha's favorite was Paris. She could shop to her heart's desire and they could stroll for hours down the boulevards. And the jewelry bargains were impossible to pass up!

Richard loved to golf and often made time for it on the weekends, except during the summer when he frequently took the yacht out. They loved to have friends on their boat and throw lavish parties. Richard and Marsha enjoyed their life. Both came from middle-class families and both were determined that their children would never feel a hunger for anything.

Their three daughters were very successful. The girls weren't each other's best friends, but they got along whenever the family was together, which was rarely.

Each had her own interests and her own set of friends. Each had her own life. The oldest was a first-year resident at a major hospital. The middle daughter had just started studying communications at an Ivy-league school, and the youngest was a junior in high school and an accomplished pianist.

Debra, the youngest, played piano from the moment she got home from school until suppertime. Nothing made her happier than playing. And being thin. She loved it when people would say, "You're so talented — and thin!" She loved it when she could brag that she had to shop in special boutiques which carried size one. She looked at herself in the mirror everyday. She would never allow one ounce of fat on her body. She would never want to lose her figure.

She was a beanpole, her best friend would tell her. Tommy had loved Debra since fourth grade and they were each other's confidants. They would share details of dates with each other and try to solve each other's problems. They were inseparable. Tommy loved being with Debra — she made him feel needed. But he hated her obsession with thinness. She talked about food and dieting constantly. She was becoming a bore. She was also making Tommy nervous.

She didn't look right lately. She seemed different, as if she were gasping for air sometimes. She didn't have energy to do anything but play the piano. And those fingers! They seemed to be a mile long, they were so bony!

Debra died just before her seventeenth birthday. She was alone in the house, playing the piano. The doctors told Richard and Marsha she had died of a heart attack. She had starved her heart for too long. The daughter who would never hunger for anything never ate anything. She weighed only 83 pounds when she died.

Sharing One's Faith

"Jesus said to them, 'If any want to become my follow-
ers, let them deny themselves and take up their cross
and follow me.' " (v. 34)

One of the greatest joys for believers is that chance to share
our faith with each other and others. The following is part of a
testimony given by Kathy Bohl, an RN from Belle Fourche, South
Dakota, to a group of representatives from Gideons International:

"I was baptized at the age of twelve, but I didn't fully understand the implications. It was just the thing to do. I asked Jesus
into my heart later one night in my bedroom. I didn't make that
step of faith public, and over the next ten years just about everything else became more important than God. Even though I let go
of him, he held onto me.

"After a couple of years out of nursing school, I joined the
Traveling Nurse Corps and on the first plane out I rededicated my
life and my career to God. Having grown up in a tiny town in rural
Pennsylvania, I wanted my first assignment to be in a big city, so I
requested Portland, Phoenix, or Boston. When the Nurse Corps
called, they asked, 'How about Colorado?' They assured me it
would only be for one month. That assignment turned out to be
permanent.

"I worked in the Intensive Care Unit in Cortez. Geographi-
cally, it is located in southwest Colorado, the only hospital for 100
miles in some directions. The town borders the Ute and Navajo
Indian reservations. There is a lot of Peyote religion and Satan
worship in the area.

"But there is a very strong Christian community as well. It
was not uncommon for one side of the family to be Peyote where
the medicine man would pray. The Christian side of the family

would go over and pray together over the patient as well. A very sweet sound to me was the American Indians praying and singing in their native language and hearing, so plainly in every few words, the name of Jesus.

"Just the presence of the Gideon Bibles in the bedside stands and the prayers that went with them meant spiritual warfare in the unit. There were many times when I could feel the presence of the Holy Spirit or the power of Satan as he fought to take lives there. I wasn't the only one. Other Christian nurses often felt the same things.

"Once I had spent a day taking care of a very ill, elderly Ute Indian gentleman. He didn't speak any English but was very restless and obviously distraught. On his window sill, I found a fan made of eagle feathers, so I asked his family what it was. They said they brought it in because he had been hearing the evil spirits calling him; because he was afraid he was going to die, the fan was there to wave away the evil spirits! A traveling nurse, a very charismatic Christian, came to relieve me after I had taken care of him. Before I could say anything to her, she said, 'You know what? Last night when I went in to take care of him, I felt my hair stand on end, and I had to pray before I could go near him!'

"One patient I shared my testimony with was Mr. B. He had chronic lung disease and because of it would retain CO_2 to life-threatening levels. He would get so sick, come into ICU, and be put on a ventilator until his levels would drop. Then he could go home for a couple of days. He had to do this several times and each time was a very miserable experience. It's really a nightmare for the patient when this occurs.

"One time he had had it. He was refusing to be put on the ventilator and told his nurse he wanted to die. I agreed to talk to him. When I went into his room, I found him sitting up in his bed breathing very fast and looking very ill. He was still coherent, so I began to talk to him about the seriousness of his illness. Then I asked him if he knew where he would go when he died. He said, 'I'm not worried about that. I've been a good man all my life. I raised good kids and was a good husband.' We talked and I read to him the gospel from the Bible.

"A very short time later his nurse found me again and this time she was very excited. She exclaimed, 'Mr. B said he's healed!' I ran with her, rather doubtingly, back to his room. Sure enough, he was sitting up on the bed looking very animated and he told me the same thing. 'I know God healed me! I had this feeling come into the top of my head and down through my body and out of my feet, and I know I'm healed!'

"We had the blood gases done early and, sure enough, his CO_2 level had dropped from 80 to 35! It was most definitely a miracle. Shortly after that, the doctor taking care of him came in. He is a Christian and the nurse and I were so excited we were both talking at once, telling him the story. He just smiled as if he already knew. I'm sure he had been praying for him.

"Mr. B's family arrived and, after sharing the story with them, we found out that they were Christian and had called out-of-town family members. We had all been praying for him at the exact time he was healed! We were so overpowered by the presence of the Holy Spirit that night and that he had allowed us to be a part of that, we could hardly function. God gave us so many people to share with that night. We prayed and praised God together."

A Second Chance

---

*"Who is wise and understanding among you? Show by
your good life that your works are done with gentle-
ness born of wisdom." (v. 13)*

Mark is a chaplain in a nursing home. He loves his job; it
gives him the feeling of doing "hands-on ministry" that was lack-
ing when he was a parish pastor. He calls his job very rewarding.

But twenty years ago, Mark's job was almost his death sentence. Mark had been so happy to get the job as nursing home
chaplain. He worked long hours, and he loved the feeling of helping and feeling needed.

The trouble was that his family needed him too. Four years
later, his wife left Mark and took their three children with her. She
cited absence and lack of interest on his part in the divorce papers.
Mark was devastated. So he worked longer hours at the home.

In those days Mark would visit as many people as he could. If
any were ill, he would often sit with them, reading scriptures or
holding their hands in prayer. He relished the stories people told
him, using many to illustrate sermon points. Mark felt connected
to these people. He loved them and was willing to serve them.

The staff on the transition unit especially loved Mark. He was
never afraid of a distraught resident. Mark always seemed to know
what to do. One technique he had to relax anxious residents was to
sit close and stroke their hair if they were lying in bed. Or he
would just hug them if they were sitting. He made them feel important and wanted. He listened to them and respected them. He
loved them.

But Mark loved them too much. He would leave after the late
shift left. He would come early and work on weekends. He didn't

mind visiting family members when a loved one died. He was everything and everywhere. He was too much.

Just before he turned 41, Mark had a heart attack. He was working and regretting the second helping of the potato dish he had earlier when he just slumped over. The doctors say it was a miracle that the custodian happened along to clean Mark's office. Mark was saved, but the doctor sat Mark down and gave him a long lecture.

The doctor, who knew Mark well, told Mark he could not return to work for six months. But before he could return, the doctor wanted assurance that Mark had learned a valuable lesson from this. He said Mark could never be so lucky to get a second chance.

Mark recuperated slowly; through his recovery period he fell into a deep depression. He didn't feel needed, he had lost his identity, and he didn't like his own company. He didn't know what to do with his "free time" and he felt worthless.

A month before he was to return to the nursing home, Mark was spending his second month in a sanitarium. But eventually Mark recovered physically, emotionally, and spiritually. The bishop encouraged him and helped him work through his suffering servant dilemma.

Mark did return to work a little over a year later. He was welcomed at the nursing home. It was a great homecoming. But Mark had learned that this was not home. This was his place of work and he was learning to take care of himself and be a servant to his personal needs also. He became a stronger chaplain because of it.

Reflections of his time surrounding the heart attack — his "second chance" as he calls it — bring tears to his eyes. He had to learn a very painful lesson. But through his pain, he has found strength. It's been almost twenty years ago and Mark is healthy. He is looking forward to retirement with his second wife, and when he says he has a time limit, there is no guilt. He has learned to serve himself.

For Or Against?

"Whoever is not against us is for us." (v. 40)

Shelley looked around and took a seat in the front row. Today was the annual meeting and she was ready to give some of these people a piece of her mind. She was sick and tired of all the changes going on. She sniffed in disgust just as Ellen walked through the door. Shelley glared at her.

Shelley hated Ellen. Ellen was a retired pastor's wife, a master of organization, very congenial, and committed to her church. And Ellen was the head of the Altar Guild. Shelley had had that job for twenty years, but now the church structure had changed and Ellen had unanimously been voted in as leader. How could they vote for someone who had only moved into the community six years ago? They didn't even know her! Surely she couldn't lead the Altar Guild as well as Shelley had!

It made Shelley really mad. Whenever she could, she made loud comments about how bad the altar looked. The cross wasn't dusted in the corner. The wax was not cut off the candles. The altar had not been polished on the side. Why, when Shelley was the leader, no usher dared step out of line. No acolyte even smiled unless Shelley told him to. And not one speck of dust was left on the cross. At least Shelley felt a little relief when people smiled at her comments.

Missy walked in and sat up front. Shelley hated Missy, too. She was the current pastor's wife. Shelley was tired of seeing Missy playing at every funeral, worship service, wedding, and social event. People were always commenting about the beautiful music Missy made. Shelley preferred the organ. They said it wasn't working, but Shelley just knew it was a lie so Missy could play the piano. Shelley would talk loudly during the preludes and postludes.

Wouldn't people rather hear Shelley's comments than Missy playing the piano — again?

Whenever Missy's daughter was around, Shelley loved to tease her. Last week Shelley had told Andrea her dress was so short that Shelley could see her underwear. And Tuesday night Andrea had worn a t-shirt over shorts at the church school carnival. Didn't Pastor Tom see how his daughter dressed these days?

And how dare Pastor Tom go on vacation and not visit Shelley's sister-in-law! They had been only seventy miles away and they didn't even call to relay Shelley's greetings! Shelley had given Pastor complete directions and phone numbers all for nothing. Pastors weren't as caring as they were fifty years ago, that was for sure.

Pastor gave devotions and an opening prayer. The council president stood up and discussed the agenda. Shelley turned to the lady next to her. The president's skirt was entirely too short and just a bit too tight. How could she sit in that dreadful thing? And the color of her shirt made her seem pale. Didn't she have a mirror? The lady didn't say anything. Shelley decided that besides her figure, her hearing must be going also.

The minutes were read and approved. The old business was reviewed and the new business was discussed. Shelley was ready when the issue of elections came up. The president was saying that those elected should be people who were committed to their church. Shelley sniffed loudly. She had attended this church for 68 years.

The president said those elected had to be people who could be looked up to and trusted. Humph, Shelley had counted the money so often, she knew by heart what the Olsons, the Skeets, and the Jameses gave every week. Did they call that tithing?

"Those who are elected need to be members of good standing, showing a record of helping, caring, and compassion, and a love for Jesus." Yeah, like who else was there the last twelve Thanksgivings when it was the church's turn to serve at the mission? Shelley sat a little taller.

The president asked if there were any other comments. Mr. Montgomery stepped up to the microphone. He was sure getting more and more hunched over, Shelley noticed. He probably sat in his recliner too much. He never did much around church. He helped usher one Sunday, but he seemed irritated when Shelley had told him he had to go home and put on a tie and clean his shoes. Thank goodness he never ushered again!

Mr. Montgomery looked at Shelley. Then he looked at the council president. "Madame President, it's nice to have those requirements, however I have just one small suggestion. We need to consider just one more thing before we nominate anyone. The person nominated should be one who builds up the body of Christ, not one who cuts it down. The person who has been for us by encouraging us to do our best in every way is for Christ. The person who acts against the body is against Christ."

A murmur went through the crowd. Shelley wondered what all that gibberish meant. The president returned to the microphone. "We will now open the floor for nominations."

May God Go With You

---

*"And he took them up in his arms, laid his hands on
them, and blessed them." (v. 16)*

Things weren't going very well. Angelica's husband's pay-check wasn't due for another week. Last month's pharmacy bill was over $200. And the emergency room had wanted cash when she brought her son in. The asthma attack couldn't have come at a worse time.

Angelica eyed the clock. Four a.m. She looked at her husband, sleeping peacefully, wishing she could sleep so soundly. She quietly rolled over and tiptoed out the room.

The recliner was comfortable and the little afghan felt good on her legs. She looked out the window and sighed. A star was twinkling overhead and the moon cast a bright glow over the yard. The swing set seemed to be in a soft spotlight. Angelica couldn't resist and went outside.

The grass felt so soft beneath her feet. The cat purred softly on the porch. She opened her eyes just long enough to make sure Angelica wasn't a stranger.

Angelica sat on a swing. She loved her yard. They had taken great pains to put in shade in just the right places. Huge pots of geraniums marked the corners. Tall corn bordered the garden to the side. She could just taste the tomatoes and cucumbers they would enjoy in a month or so.

She took a deep breath. Ahh, the night seemed to have a perfume to it. Maybe it was the eucalyptus trees growing to the south. Or perhaps it was the gardenias. The tea olive was in bloom. It was her favorite scent of all as it blew through the house on a warm summer day.

Her children loved to play here. Their friends filled the yard on many holidays. Family members would spill over the lawns at every celebration. It was a lively, fun place.

Yet it was a quiet, magical place too. Angelica loved to read novels on the hammock on Sunday afternoons. And gardening was her quiet time. Her time to think about things, to ask God to give her strength and to give her direction. It was a blessed spot. She bowed her head and asked for God's presence in the days ahead. She asked for guidance in making decisions. And she thanked God for the many blessings in her life. There were so many! How could she even begin to count them all? Children, a faithful husband, loyal friends, and a close family. She would make it because God would be with her.

She crept back into the kitchen noiselessly. As she turned to close the door, her eye caught a postcard. She had bought it at a restored Norwegian stave church while on vacation during better times. It read:

As you go on your way, May God go with you.
May He go before you to show you the way;
May He go behind you to encourage you;
Beside you to befriend you;
Above you to watch over you;
And within you to give you peace.

Angelica did feel peace — a peace of knowing God was with her, a peace of knowing that, all in all, things would work out.

Trust In God

---

*"... go, sell what you own, and give the money to the
poor, and you will have treasure in heaven...." (v. 21)*

Jancy counted her money. No matter how she looked at it,
there was no money for the glasses her daughter needed. And the
brakes that were already grinding would have to be fixed next
month. Her extra money from this paycheck had gone toward the
new basketball uniform her son needed.

She tried to analyze their situation. They were all very healthy.
She was grateful her garden was growing so well. They didn't
need meat. But why was it so difficult?

She put her head in her hands. How would they make it? How
long could she live on the edge, going from paycheck to paycheck
with barely anything left over? Maybe she should get a third part-
time job.

But that didn't seem right. She wanted to spend time with her
two children. And her husband assured her they would be able to
make it once the loan was paid off. She would have to trust him.

And she did. A few years later they were able to move into a
small house, and they had a margin. A margin for emergencies, for
small family vacations, and a margin to tithe more for offering.

Jancy trusted her husband and trusted God to help her. Times
were not always easy, but she had held on. And they made it. She
understood what it was like to have to use a calculator and put
things back in the grocery store before she could check out. She
knew what it was like to want a new dress for a special occasion
only to wear an old dress. She knew the taste of economical din-
ners very well.

But Jancy had grown from her experience, and she taught her
children about money. She taught them to tithe. Every week she

would pass out their allowance and watch as they put one third in the "church" slot, one third in the "bank" slot, and the final third in the "for fun" slot. Early she taught them the value of saving and the responsibility of having money.

When Jancy and her husband retired, they began giving anonymous scholarships. At first they were little amounts, but as their children became successful and more independent, they felt freer to give more. And the scholarships became bigger and bigger.

Jancy came to see that God gave her money to be used wisely, for church and for service. She felt fortunate to have the resources to do that. She felt it a responsibility to share. But mostly, she felt great joy in giving back what was first given her.

One Pastor's Story

---

*"... but whoever wishes to become great among you
must be your servant...." (v. 43)*

Craig Barnes has learned what it is to be a servant. And he
knows what it is like to serve. He knows firsthand what it is like to
be forgotten, left behind. And he knows what it is like to be a
leader and looked up to.

When Craig was a teen, his mother left her husband and two
sons. Craig's father, a pastor, was asked to resign from his posi-
tion. His father left the church and his sons. Craig, who was sixteen, and his older brother were left to take care of themselves.
They sold their parents' belongings and did their best.

As their first Christmas alone approached, the boys thought
they could hitchhike to see their mother. They set out on a cold
night, only to be told by a police officer that the road had been
closed two hours earlier. They felt despair. They felt abandoned.
And they recalled a passage that reminded them that though they
had nothing, they had been called by God, named by God, and
loved by God.

Craig remembers feeling very low, very distraught. He dropped
out after a year of college and started pumping gas at midnight. He
knew this wasn't what God had intended for him. A pastor, John
Wallon, befriended Craig and encouraged him in his faith. It was
life-giving. Craig graduated from King's College and married Anne,
his high school sweetheart.

Craig went on to seminary at Princeton and he and Anne became parents of Lyndsey, who is now seventeen. His first call was
to First Presbyterian Church in Colorado Springs, Colorado. Three
years later he took a leave and went to the University of Chicago
for a doctorate in church history before returning to Colorado.

Craig took another call to Wisconsin and five years later his life changed. National Presbyterian in Washington, D.C., the closest thing to a cathedral for the Presbyterian (U.S.A.) Church, invited him to be their pastor. Craig was 36. Only nine days later, Craig received another call: the doctor told Craig he had thyroid cancer.

Anne and Craig were drawn to Washington, but they had to deal with Craig's illness, surgery, and treatments. Nevertheless, they went to Washington. Full of enthusiasm, full of cancer, and full of hope.

National has been blessed with the Barnes' presence since 1993. Craig still has to take leave each January for radiation therapy, but he feels his weaknesses from his childhood have given him strength to understand and preach grace, something Anne and Craig had to learn firsthand. They bring hope to others when others seem to have lost it all. Craig had lost it all at one time, yet he knew who was Lord. He knew whom to serve.

(Details taken from the article "Barnes Ennobled" in *Pastor's Family*, August/September 1998.)

Proper 25
Job 42:1-6, 10-17

Salvador's Testimony

"The Lord blessed the latter days of Job more than his
beginning...." (v. 12)

Salvador has a scar on his cheek that runs alongside his eye, from chin to forehead. When he was three, his brother was carrying him, and he tripped against the fence of the horse corral. They were on their way to feed the horses and were eager to finish. Salvador fell into the pen and a horse stepped on him, spooked by Salvador's sudden movement.

Although Salvador suffered great pain, he had miraculously escaped eye injury and brain damage from the huge animal's step. He healed well, though the scar was not stitched well. It was a ragged line, pinched in places. The scar was obvious even from a distance.

In his younger years, he was very self-conscious about the scar on his face. He tried makeup to hide it once, but he didn't think it looked natural. He tried to be quiet and reserved, but that wasn't how God made him. Salvador loved people; he was outgoing and he loved to talk.

When Salvador became a successful public speaker, he always brought up the accident and his scar. "You can't hide something like that," he would say. "That would be like trying to hide a third leg." Salvador chose instead to be open about it. He used his scar to point to God. He used it as a testimony.

But he didn't always have that confidence. When Salvador was in his early elementary days, the children had called him "monster" and "scarface." It had been very painful to see friends turn on him and join in with others to make fun of him. Salvador had wanted to run away at times, but in a small town, it was not possible. He had been forced to face the children. He had to make peace about what had happened to him.

He had found strength in that knowledge. Salvador was able to accept his face and his appearance. And he used it to point to God's miracles and overcoming negativity. Salvador triumphed from his fate in that he understood prejudice and discrimination. He had knowledge that he couldn't hide.

Where You Go, I Will Go

*"But Ruth said, 'Do not press me to leave you or to
turn back from following you! Where you go, I will go;
where you lodge, I will lodge; your people shall be my
people, and your God my God.' " (v. 16)*

Riley loved her family. She was very close to her parents and
sisters and brothers. She adored her in-laws, enjoying family get-
togethers on both sides. She felt she had a happy life.

Riley and her husband John had been married five years when
John was given the opportunity to live and work in a new region.
He would head up a new department and be given a handsome
raise. There was promise of future promotions and the company
would see that he would be moved into a dream house in style.

Job security, more responsiblity, and a chance to shine: it was
everything John had wanted. And nothing Riley wanted a part of.
She saw it as a death sentence: distance from family and friends,
the loss of her job and everything dear to her. But John was more
dear to her. She agonized at the thought, but she decided she had
to follow John.

Riley's family said their tearful farewells with promises of visiting soon. Friends came with little gifts so she could remember
them. But she reminded them they had the telephone and electronic mail. They could all keep in touch, just not touch as often.
She and John made the move.

At first it was very difficult. The region was very unfamiliar
and at times Riley felt stupid, asking for help with simple survival
skills. She had to learn to manipulate the propane tank, drive on
ice, and deal with insects.

But Riley felt John was worth every ounce of it. Loyalty to
John was only a small price to pay for the loyalty John had to

Riley. It was a rare quality. It was a treasured quality. Riley had to see this through.

With time Riley saw how lucky she was. She didn't need to work and she had time to play her instruments. She started a small orchestra to play during worship. She found many friends in her musical circles.

Riley and John had children: two boys in five years. The children thrived. Riley found new interests and finally grew peaceful with the move. She felt it was worth it. Family and friends still come to visit and the telephone and electronic mail are daily habits. She feels she has been rewarded for her loyalty.

A Widow's Might

"A poor widow came and put in two small copper coins...." (v. 42)

Ada's husband had died three years ago. The journey through grief was a long road, but she was making progress. She didn't awake thinking her husband Arnold was standing in front of her anymore. She didn't cry out in loneliness so often anymore. She was healing, although she knew in a way she would always need healing.

Ada was getting restless. She wanted to return to the active social schedule she had had with Arnold. But she needed a safe place to socialize.

Ada moved to be closer to her daughter. She liked the town, but she didn't know many people — until a neighbor offered Ada a ride to church with her. Ruth, who was also a widow, had heard Ada had moved to the neighborhood and invited herself over with cookies one day. She told Ada about the busy church across town where she attended. They shared and laughed and started a friendship that day.

Ada lived three doors down from Ruth and they spent much time together. Ruth introduced Ada to all kinds of people and soon Ada had a full calendar. But Tuesday was always reserved for Ruth. They had a standing lunch date, a group came over for a card game, and then they all had dinner. They had a wonderful time.

One of Ada's interests had always been art and sewing. When the church had a need for banners for the lounge, Ada recruited Ruth to help cut and pin. Ada made beautiful banners, designed with simplicity and drama. Ada dragged Ruth along to the craft bazaars and soon Ada formed a small group to make projects. She inspired them to make projects all year and donate them for sale at the church bazaar.

Ada was busy and always giving of her time. Her pension wasn't very big, but it was just big enough for her to manage the upkeep on her house. Besides, she needed money to keep her passion alive. She always found ways to integrate art into whatever she was doing.

Ada designed a funeral pall in time for the dedication of the new sanctuary. Two matching banners had been crafted for their permanent home on each side of the enormous cross hanging against the back wall. Signs were needlepointed to instruct visitors where the restrooms, office, and points of interest were.

Ada stenciled the wall of the new bathrooms. On the doors, matching wreaths hung above embroidered signs. Nothing "new" for Ada remained untouched by her love of handcrafting.

When babies were baptized, it was Ada who embroidered a tiny cross in peach and light green at the corner of a hanky. New members got a small quilt with the name of the church embroidered in the center. After funerals, Ada made flowers from the ribbon of the bouquets, giving one to each member of the family to keep.

On cold nights, Ada could take a tiny bit of comfort knowing that many of the homeless were wearing scarves or mittens her group gathered to crochet every Monday evening. So many projects — so much energy! And all from one woman!

Ada kept up her pace in her new environment for thirteen years until her health declined. At her funeral, friends spoke of a tiny woman, full of ideas, full of energy, and full of initiative. Ada didn't have much money, but she had might. A widow's might that gave warmth, comfort, treasures, and beauty to others for generations to come.

God Was On Her Side

"But Hannah answered, 'No, my Lord, I am a woman deeply troubled ... Do not regard your servant as a worthless woman, for I have been speaking out of my great anxiety and vexation all this time.'" (vv. 15-16)

Brianna was nervous. This was a big step for her. One of the biggest steps she would ever take.

She didn't really know what she was in for, but she knew she had to do it. It was going to be a monumental undertaking and an even greater task to keep up, but the rewards would outweigh the risks. Brianna was excited.

The clock said 5 a.m. Three more hours and it would begin. Another dimension to her life. Another life. Brianna looked at her sleeping husband. Quietly, she got up, brushed her teeth, and looked at her devotion card for the day.

"I sought the Lord and he heard me, and delivered me from all my fears" (Psalm 34:4).

It was perfect. She was nervous. This was a big day. But God was on her side.

Brianna sang in the shower and then considered her devotion. Yes, the Lord knew she was nervous. The Lord had heard her fears. The Lord would deliver her. This was a new opportunity. A new beginning. And she would not be alone.

Three hours later, she and her husband stood at the doorway, nervous but excited. They were ready to go through the door. Ready for an awesome burden. Ready for a lifetime of rewards, tribulation, and memories. Ready for the new daughter they would adopt today.

Seeing With New Eyes

"... they are now justified by his grace as a gift, through the redemption that is in Christ Jesus...." (v. 24)

Rudy looked around. He couldn't believe it. It had finally ended. He was free. Rudy practically skipped down the long hall to his lawyer, who was waiting to drive him home.

Two years in prison was two years too long for him. Being in the wrong place at the wrong time, a false accusation, and wrongful conviction had led to two years of lost time. Two years of being treated as an animal with no personality. Two years of living under constant supervision, with no privacy whatsoever.

It had been a long two years, but Rudy had worked hard with his lawyer until the real criminal was apprehended. His lawyer had warned him that Rudy would be a changed man on the "outside." But Rudy couldn't wait. He wanted freedom. He could just taste it. For two long years that was all he had thought about.

The transition was very difficult. Rudy couldn't sleep very well. He couldn't get used to the quiet of his suburban neighborhood. Had it always been so peaceful?

His wife and family seemed the same, but Rudy had changed. He saw everything through the eyes of a captive. He knew he needed help.

It took another two years of intense counseling, first with Rudy and then with the family as a whole, until Rudy felt comfortable enough to be his old self. But he knew he could never really be his old self. Gone were quick dismissals of people. Gone was the ungrateful heart he had once had. Gone was the cynicism.

Rudy saw everything with new eyes. He saw the hard work of the waitress. He told the school janitor how much he appreciated his constant supervision of the school grounds. He shared his story with the teachers so they could understand. He never wanted any of his staff or the students to feel trapped, convicted, or judged. Rudy never wanted anyone to feel that way while he was principal.

For years after his imprisonment, Rudy shared with anyone he could about his experience in prison. In church, at the school, and to any group who would have him, Rudy shared the unbelievable oppression of prison.

Rudy was free now. He was able to feel gratitude, humor, hurt, and happiness once again. It was great to be able to have an opinion that mattered.

He was free. Free to be himself. Free just to be!

All Saints' Sunday
Revelation 21:1-6a

God's Presence In The Millennium

*"Then I saw a new heaven and a new earth; for the
first heaven and the first earth had passed away...."*
(v. 1)

The speaker was funny, interesting, engaging, and very knowledgeable. She was telling about Revelation in the face of the millennium. Would the world end at the turn of the millennium? As a pastor, lecturer, and professor, she had many stories to tell and many observations about people in general. The whole concept of the millennium was fascinating.

We heard about the commercialism surrounding the millennium. Only so many shopping days left ... Only 2,000 of these will be made ... Only this many will be made until the millennium ... And we heard of the fanatics who feel that at the turn of the "odometer" of time, things will just end, or blow up, or who knows what fate will deliver.

The lecturer had statistics, poetry, cartoons, and research to support the case that the world would go on as usual on January 1, 2000. But psychologically, things will be different, she said. It will be another century, another millennium, another milestone for the earth. We will see things a bit differently, she assured us, just because of the numbers.

But she also assured us that God will still be there, no matter what the date on the calendar says. To God it won't be a milestone. God has another calendar, another space in time.

It was a brilliant lecture. A brilliant argument for the status quo. She called for questions.

Leon stood up. He didn't exactly have a question, he said. But he had an observation to make. "I appreciate all you have said about a new milestone, a new millennium, a new era. But my millennium came on April 19, 1997, when my town was flooded. We were supposed to evacuate, but I couldn't leave. I watched as water rushed down the street toward us. I watched water fill the basement and much of the main floor. I watched as the flood soaked up and carried off my possessions. I watched and my soul cried out in disbelief.

"I watched as the National Guard carried us off in helicopters. I watched as the damage was assessed three weeks later when the water finally receded. I watched and I cried out in pain.

"I watched as Salvation Army trucks brought us food three times a day. I watched young people from across the nation come and muck out our homes. I watched the letter carrier bring boxes that were simply addressed to 'flood victims.'

"People I didn't even know carried away our waterlogged belongings. People I didn't even know carried in new belongings that had been donated by churches, corporations, schools, clubs, and ordinary people. I watched as people helped me rebuild and renew.

"I watched God's presence in the aftermath of the flood. That was my millennium. That was the beginning of a new era for me. That was the time God's presence was made known to me."

We Gather Together

"The Lord has done great things for us, and we rejoiced." (v. 3)

The aromas were inviting. Turkey, dressing, gravy, and cranberries. Mashed potatoes and sweet potatoes, green beans and corn. Pecan, pumpkin, and apple pies. It all looked so good. It all smelled so delicious.

Floral arrangements were scattered throughout the house. Roses from the garden adorned the dinner table. Fruit and pine cones spilled out of a basket by the door. A cornucopia held nuts and small fruit on the mantel. Their smells and colors were intoxicating.

There was a quiet in the house. The children were getting dressed. The oven was keeping the food warm and the table was neatly set. Glasses had been wiped, crystal bowls had been filled, and linen napkins were intricately folded. Everything was ready.

This was Thanksgiving. A day to eat. A day to lounge around. A day to share with family and friends.

The doorbell rang and a steady stream of people entered the house. The quiet had come to an end. Children bounded downstairs and gave squeals of delight at the arrival of cousins. Grownups exchanged greetings and gave fruit, a bottle of wine, and other little gifts. Everyone was in a festive mood. Talk was constant and the volume was up.

Grandpa rang the tiny copper bell from the mantel. No one seemed to notice. He rang it again and the room grew quiet. "Gather around. We're going to have our meal, but we can't begin until everyone has given thanks for something in their life. Who would like to start?"

Round and round everyone gave thanks for something. Little Andy gave thanks for his new birthday present last week: a big fire truck that had lights that blinked! Rachel gave thanks for her first-born son. Ellie thanked God for eighty healthy years. Matt gave thanks for his new job. Everyone had a chance. Everyone gave thanks.

This was Thanksgiving. A day to eat. A day to lounge around. A day to share with family and friends. A time to articulate the gratitude each felt.

Christ The King
John 18:33-37

The Message Of The Cross

"Then Pilate ... asked him, 'Are you the King of the Jews?' " (v. 33)

"Can you make a banner for the church?"

Leanna trembled. She loved to sew and make banners, but what should she make? This was a huge church and the canvas would be large. Many, many people would see it. This was a chance to share the gospel in one dramatic instance. It had to be just right.

Images which were bold and uncomplicated were Leanna's trademark. The banner would be up most of the year and she was given carte blanche: it could be her idea, her creation, her message. After much prayer, she started researching the possibilities.

One day Leanna sketched a pelican. The symbol of piety, a pelican will tear open her own breast to feed her young in times of famine. The pelican had three baby pelicans at her breast. It was a serene picture but Leanna wasn't satisfied. People might not see the connection.

Thinking of birds, Leanna drew a peacock. Resurrection, renewal, and immortality were on Leanna's mind as she used purple, orange, blues, greens, and yellows on the body. But when she stepped back, she saw vanity and pride in the stance and tilt of his head. It wasn't the message she wanted to convey.

One morning Leanna was inspired to draw a perfect rose. Pinks turned to a deep shade of red. Tightly wound petals uncurled around the edge of the rose. It was lovely, but it wasn't quite right.

After a short jog around the park, Leanna penciled a bunch of grapes and a cluster of wheat. Christ in the wine and bread. How fitting during Holy Communion! It was a beautiful picture with deep purples and browns, but it was too predictable. It wasn't what Leanna had in mind. It lacked drama for her taste.

Two days later, Leanna was particularly excited with her rendition of a knee with young children on it. The children's faces were tilted upward, listening to an unseen speaker. An arm was around them. It was a compassionate scene. But it still wasn't the message she wanted to convey.

She toyed with the idea of a cross, but how surprising was that? It would also be predictable and common. It wouldn't be dramatic. But the thought wouldn't leave her and she sketched crosses in different angles. Finally she settled on the upper half of a rugged cross, splinters showing on the edges. She drew a trace of shoulders with a head hanging down. But it was very vague. Were the shoulders a figment of the imagination or were they really there? It was just the effect Leanna wanted. But something was missing.

The rough cross filled up the entire canvas, and the eyes were drawn to the faint outline of shoulders stretching from side to side. She drew the thinnest circle resting on the one of the shoulders, adding small nettles. But she made them look like long ovals. One had to look hard. Were they thorns or jewels? It was perfect. It was finished. It was just what Leanna had in mind. She couldn't wait to start sewing as she considered the image before her.

It was only on the rough cross that Jesus became Lord, the final authority, the king. On that day it was perfect. It was finished.